The Changing Face of Burberry

The Changing Face of Burberry

Britishness, Heritage, Labour and Consumption

Siân Weston

BLOOMSBURY VISUAL ARTS
LONDON • NEW YORK • OXFORD • NEW DELHI • SYDNEY

BLOOMSBURY VISUAL ARTS
Bloomsbury Publishing Plc
50 Bedford Square, London, WC1B 3DP, UK
1385 Broadway, New York, NY 10018, USA
29 Earlsfort Terrace, Dublin 2, Ireland

BLOOMSBURY, BLOOMSBURY VISUAL ARTS and the Diana logo are
trademarks of Bloomsbury Publishing Plc

First published in Great Britain 2023
Paperback edition published by Bloomsbury Visual Arts 2024

Cover design by Adriana Brioso
Cover image: Kate Moss for Burberry, SS 2001 © MARIO TESTINO/Art Partner

A catalogue record for this book is available from the British Library.

A catalog record for this book is available from the Library of Congress.

ISBN: HB: 978-1-3501-7960-8
PB: 978-1-3503-3221-8
ePDF: 978-1-3501-7961-5
eBook: 978-1-3501-7962-2

Typeset by Newgen KnowledgeWorks Pvt. Ltd., Chennai, India

To find out more about our authors and books visit www.bloomsbury.com
and sign up for our newsletters.

In memory of my lovely parents Ray and Lyn Weston

Contents

List of Figures   viii

Acknowledgements   xi

Introduction   1

1   A one-hundred-and-fifty-year metamorphosis   9

2   A new rose   37

3   Surviving through Britishness   51

4   Good and bad consumers: The lost fight and the fight back   73

5   The £13,000 handbag   103

6   Heritage, craft and the global marketplace   125

Conclusions   159

Bibliography   165

Index   181

Figures

1.1   Thomas Burberry's store in Church Street Basingstoke, 1910.
      Image © Hampshire County Council. Image provided by
      Hampshire Cultural Trust   10
1.2   Lord Kitchener in a Burberry 'Tielocken', 1916. Image provided
      by Mary Evans Picture Library   12
1.3   Frank Hurley, photographer on Sir Earnest Shackleton's
      expedition to the Antarctic 1914, dressed in Burberry
      clothing. Image provided by Getty Images (Royal
      Geographical Society)   15
1.4   Swan and Edgar's department store, Regent Street, 1914. Image
      provided by Getty Images (Hulton Archive)   18
1.5   Burberry store, Haymarket London 1913 designed by
      Walter Cave. Image provided by RIBA Collections   19
1.6   Burberry officer uniform, the First World War.
      Image provided by Amoret Tanner and Alamy Stock Photos   20
1.7   Employees at Burberry's factory, Basingstoke, possibly
      celebrating 1918 Armistice. Image © Hampshire County
      Council. Image provided by Hampshire Cultural Trust   23
1.8   Burberry specialist ski clothes, 1925. Image provided by the
      Advertising Archives; all clothes and accessories by
      Burberry   26
1.9   Burberry advertisement in *The Graphic*, March 1930. Image
      provided by Mary Evans Picture Library   27
1.10 Burberry in *Country Life* coronation special, June 1953. Image
      provided by Mary Evans Picture Library   30
1.11 Burberry cotton houndstooth coat, the *Tatler*, January 1959.
      Photograph by Michael Molinari; image © Illustrated London
      News Ltd. Provided by Mary Evans Picture Library   32
2.1   Hugh Dancy for Burberry Brit, 2003. Photograph © Mario
      Testino. Image provided by Art Partner New York; all clothes
      and accessories by Burberry   39

2.2   Burberry Beijing, 2011. Photograph by Ian Gavan. Image
provided by Getty Images; all clothes and accessories by Burberry   45

3.1   Kate Moss for Burberry, Autumn–Winter 2005. Photograph ©
Mario Testino. Image provided by Art Partner New York; all
clothes and accessories by Burberry   52

3.2   Stella Tennant for Burberry, 1998. Photograph © Mario Testino.
Image provided by Art Partner New York; all clothes and
accessories by Burberry   57

3.3   Stella Tennant for Burberry, 2000. Photograph © Mario Testino
Image provided by Art Partner New York; all clothes and
accessories by Burberry   60

3.4   Kate Moss for Burberry, Spring–Summer 2001. Photograph ©
Mario Testino. Image provided by Art Partner New York; all
clothes and accessories by Burberry   61

3.5   Kate Moss for Burberry, Autumn–Winter 2004. Photograph ©
Mario Testino. Image provided by Art Partner New York; all
clothes and accessories by Burberry   67

4.1   Kate Moss and Liberty Ross for Burberry, Spring–Summer 2000.
Photograph © Mario Testino. Image provided by Art Partner
New York; all clothes and accessories by Burberry   74

4.2   Convicted Scuttler William Brooks (1870). Image provided by
Greater Manchester Police Museum and Archive   79

6.1   Gabriella Wilde and Roo Panes for Burberry, Autumn–Winter
2012. Photograph © Mario Testino. Image provided by Art
Partner New York; all clothes and accessories by Burberry   126

6.2   Lily Donaldson for Burberry, Autumn–Winter 2004. Photograph
© Mario Testino. Image provided by Art Partner New York; all
clothes and accessories by Burberry   128

6.3   Gemma Ward for Burberry, Spring–Summer 2006. Photograph
© Mario Testino. Image provided by Art Partner New York; all
clothes and accessories by Burberry   132

6.4   Lily Donaldson, Keira Gormley and Agyness Deyn for Burberry,
Autumn–Winter 2007. Photograph © Mario Testino. Image
provided by Art Partner New York; all clothes and accessories by
Burberry   134

6.5   Lily Donaldson for Burberry Prorsum, Spring–Summer 2009.
Photograph © Mario Testino. Image provided by Art Partner
New York; all clothes and accessories by Burberry   136

6.6   Look 36 Burberry Prorsum Men's Wear, Autumn–Winter 2009.
       Image provided by ImaxTree, Milan; all clothes and accessories
       by Burberry   142
6.7   Burberry Prorsum at London Fashion Week, Autumn–Winter
       2010. Photograph by Ian Gavan. Image provided by Getty
       Images; all clothes and accessories by Burberry   144
6.8   Betty Kirby-Green and Flying Officer Arthur Clouston with
       Burberry plane, 1937. Image provided by Mary Evans
       Picture Library   148

Acknowledgements

Although my name stands alone as author of this book, it has been a collaborative endeavour and I'd like to thank the following people and organizations for their support.

Professor Beverley Skeggs for her unceasing encouragement and undimmed confidence in my research work. GMB officer Mervyn Burnett and former Burberry machinists Joan Young and her co-workers Leigh Johnson and Anne Jones for helping me to complete such an engaging period of primary research.

I'd particularly like to thank Mario Testino for supplying important images for this publication; Alice Bowring, studio manager at Mario Testino and Stefanie Breslin at Art Partner New York.

Special thanks to Annabelle Campbell and the Crafts Council for awarding me a Spark Plug curators' award which funded *Can Craft Make You Happy?* with artists Bedwyr Williams and Deirdre Nelson, in a piece of research that embedded creative risk. Sam Butcher at the Hampshire Cultural Trust and Alison Carter, formerly at Hampshire Museum Services, and in memory of David Quelch, the Burberry Archivist.

Many thanks to the agencies who kindly gave image permissions including

Lucy Baxter at KMA representing Kate Moss
Natalie Hand at Viva London model management representing Stella Tennant, and in memory of Ms Tennant
Elizabeth Carpenter and Daniel Naval at IMG representing Lily Donaldson and Gemma Ward
Fraser Belk at Established Models representing Kiera Gormley
Erin King at the Independent Talent Group representing Agyness Deyn
Cory Bautista at New York Model Management representing Liberty Ross
Alexandra Rae at United Artists representing Hugh Dancy
Sian Steel at Tess Management representing Gabriella Wilde
Julie Thorp at CRC Music representing Roo Panes

I also want to extend my thanks to:

Katie Henderson at the Greater Manchester Police Museum and Archive

Vera Zennaro at ImaxTree

Lucinda Gosling and Mark Braund at the Mary Evans Picture Library

Jonathan Makepeace at the Royal Institute of British Architects (RIBA) Library

To my wonderful friends Helen Carnac, Linda Sandino, James Bosley, Faye McNulty and Kay Politowicz for their ongoing support throughout my research.

Finally, I'd like to extend my thanks to Frances Arnold at Bloomsbury Academic for her unending and positive support during the production of this manuscript. It's been quite a journey.

The reproduction of images from The Hampshire Cultural Trust, Advertising Archives and Mary Evans Picture Library were funded with generous support from the University for the Creative Arts Research School.

Every effort has been made to trace copyright holders and to accurately attribute authorship of images reproduced within this book. The author wants to make it clear that this publication has no association with Burberry plc., and the content is not endorsed by them.

Introduction

The Changing Face of Burberry offers new material on the diffusion of a luxury fashion brand; it examines Burberry's use of heritage and questions whether consumption and luxury have crossed class lines. The scope of this research runs from the historic beginnings of the company in 1856, until Chief Creative Officer Christopher Bailey leaves the company in 2018, and these distinct temporal contexts encourage an examination of the radical changes to fashion production and retail over three centuries. Burberry's changing identity is set against a background that runs from an era when garments were made by a single hand, through two world wars, and what Wally Olins (1978) described as new trading communities in the 1970s, to the information age in the late twentieth and early twenty-first century, where we see a digitized and global marketplace where many consumers have a purely online relationship with the brand.

Burberry is a rich source for fashion scholars and is arguably one of Britain's most legendary fashion companies, and although it is widely covered and largely applauded in the financial press and fashion media, very little has been written about it from a theoretical perspective. *The Changing Face of Burberry* aims to fill this gap in the literature by examining the company from multiple perspectives, including its history and cultural identity in both national and international contexts, examining the ways in which the company constructs its own specialist vernacular in areas including Britishness, heritage and labour. It also considers how for a few years in the early twenty-first century, the company fell prey to the intricacies of the British class system which led to instances of contested consumption.

The text aims to determine how this historic company rose from a semi-rural, craft-based industry in the nineteenth century to become a global fashion brand and cultural object in the twenty-first century. It questions how this British brand has been able to captivate millennials in contemporary consumer culture, and asks why these customers are in thrall to a brand with more than a one-hundred-and-fifty-year history. And, more specifically, what attracts young international consumers to narratives of Britishness? The text explores these questions by examining the history of the company to determine how it has used its considerable lifespan to develop a brand that is reassuringly stable, particularly to younger consumers, many of whom may be overwhelmed by the digitized, always-on consumer landscape. However, it also asks why although Burberry positions itself within the luxury market, its geographic entanglement with Britain has meant that its meaning remains mobile, which is simultaneously precarious, contradictory and paradoxical.

The sharp subject focus is complemented by a broad range of research approaches, including interviews with factory workers, examination of archive materials and historical government documents, image analysis of Burberry adverts from the nineteenth to the twenty-first century and consumer responses from online resources and social media platforms. Two archives formed important resources for the development of this research, one belonging to Burberry and another to the Hampshire Cultural Trust. The Burberry archive was particularly difficult to access, and after a long and protracted process, my eventual gatekeeper was the Keeper of Art & Design at Hampshire Museum Services (now the Hampshire Cultural Trust), who introduced me to the archivist at Burberry, David Quelch. Quelch had been appointed after his retirement as director of sister company, the Scotch House. I visited the archive when he was rebuilding the company's records, as so little of its past had been kept, a paradoxical state of affairs given that Burberry now rely so heavily on the archive as a central design direction. Quelch invited me to visit the archive again, and though his offer was generous, my access to this archive was short term as he died shortly after our first meeting. I thought about Antoinette Burton's (2006) description of the bureaucratic nature of archival encounters, where she argues that stories are limited by the administration of the archive, as this had effectively halted my research. My archive fever stemmed not from an anxiety concerning the ethics of the archive, but from a lack of archive. My experience at the Hampshire Cultural Trust was its polar opposite, and I visited their premises at Chilcomb House in Winchester a number of times over a ten-year period. I watched as their archive became more professionalized and detailed through digitization, and now houses photographs, financial records, historical marketing materials, garments and accessories, and materials from this archive are used throughout this text.

My focus on Burberry emerged through two important sources – one a professional scenario and another wholly connected to my family. In the first scenario, whilst I was working at the now-defunct London Printworks Trust, based in Brixton, south London, I developed and co-delivered a five-week design project called *World Cup 98*, co-funded by Arts Council England. This was in May 1998, and I worked with a group of teenagers, half of whom were described as young people at risk of offending. This culturally diverse group designed and printed five-a-side football strips, played in a knock out football tournament, and edited a specially commissioned fanzine. I was curious about their dress as many of the boys proudly wore Burberry scarves, jackets and baseball caps that they steadfastly refused to remove, despite the hot and messy studio conditions. But this scenario was not an unusual one, as my background as a specialist curator for fashion and textiles has brought me into contact with other marginalized groups whose interest in luxury clothing brands was a strong element of their identity formation. But the focus on Burberry as a *group* identity was new to me, and it became clear that this group used the Burberry Nova check as a way of signalling a tacit connection to one another, despite the potentially adversarial scenario of competition in both the design stages and the knock-out tournament: *World Cup 98* successfully demonstrated a clear bond between Burberry wearers, however these consumers seemed far from the company's ideal target market, as they were from low-income, working-class families, a demographic that was distant from Burberry's socially elite image, and I began to question how these young consumers had found their way to the brand.

My interest in Burberry and its connections to an apparent polarity of class and age remained, and when in 2006 the company announced the closure of its Treorchy production plant in the Rhondda Valley, this added another layer of complexity to Burberry's story – one that involved industrial relations and brand transparency, as press interest in the closure mounted and the company was heavily scrutinized. That the plant was in Wales, homeland to both my mother and grandmother, tipped the balance for me, particularly as both these women used craft skills to make clothes and household textiles. And indeed, my grandmother's experience as a Norwegian immigrant was eased through her brilliance at making, and craft became what I'd describe as her settlement language. This skill formed a strong core of female pride, not only as a source of technical excellence, but one of thrift. I tried to visualize what it meant for the largely female workforce in Treorchy to go from using complex craft skills to make high-quality luxury garments, and how this might feel now they were no longer required, or paid, to make this clothing, and had lost their livelihood.

Within my own scholarship at art school studying fashion and textiles, I examined class structure through dress and adornment, and subsequently my research focused on consumption practices, and I became interested in textiles as political objects. This focus came alive when I began to consider the closure of the Treorchy plant in parallel to my family's experience: one of fitting in, and one of thrift, and this led me to develop an oral history project called *Can Craft Make You Happy?* which was funded by the Crafts Council. This allowed me to travel to Wales to develop primary research materials with some of the former machinists at the Burberry plant in Treorchy. *Can Craft Make You Happy?* examined what it was like to make clothing for the luxury fashion industry, while being unable to be a consumer in that sector. It considered issues around women's labour, social structures in the workplace and the reality of losing a job in an area of high unemployment, and this research has essentially informed the empirical elements of this book.

The footballing teens inform another large section of the text, that of the 'bad' consumer. In 1998, I found the students to be engaged and creative and, at the time, my only question focused on why they'd selected Burberry as their uniform of choice, as we were still some six years away from a miniature moral panic in the British print and broadcast media, which linked working class Burberry consumers to lawlessness. Could this be traced back to a time in the 1950s when Burberry's identity became diffused and separated from its luxury profile, when goods produced by the company were sold through a mail-order catalogue, seen during this era as an element of working-class consumer culture?

Over the course of my research, two further elements emerged: the nature and value of Britishness, and how Burberry utilizes heritage as a capital-producing element of the contemporary brand, and these were developed through forensic examination of Burberry's marketing materials and press coverage from the outset of the company in the mid-nineteenth century up until 2018. *The Changing Face of Burberry* includes analysis on how two North American CEOs, Rose Marie Bravo and Angela Ahrendts, developed Burberry from the mid-1990s onwards into what is now widely viewed as *the* quintessential British brand using narratives in their marketing campaigns that include shoplifting, horse riding and a Pearly King & Queen. Their choice of models in the early campaigns – the street-wise Kate Moss and the aristocratic Stella Tennant – are used to show how differing forms of Britishness were used to sell an idealized discourse of British identity, particularly to consumers outside the nation state.

As the information age matured in the twenty-first century, Burberry's online output and activity are used to show how they used images of the past to sell a romanticized form of old England, but with additions in the form of hip young models and tastemakers including Agyness Deyn, Cara Delevigne, Lily

Donaldson and Hugh Dancy. Burberry's online initiatives, Runway to Reality, Art of the Trench and Burberry Acoustic show how the brand started to capture the imagination and buying power of young international consumers by inviting them to live runway shows and behind-the-scenes pre-runway exclusives, in what were previously exclusive VIP-only events. This heady mix, coupled with references to the Bloomsbury Group, the Duke and Duchess of Windsor, Shackleton's Antarctic expeditions and the Second World War cadet girls, helped to embed the romance of heritage in to the contemporary Burberry brand.

These developments within fashion production and dissemination are underpinned by an examination of political and industrial changes including a huge shift in post-war consumerism, the erosion of heavy industry in the United States and Britain in the 1980s, and its replacement by the service sector, of which fashion retail plays a large part. The election of a New Labour government in the mid-1990s, the expansion of the Chinese economy and their thirst for luxury European fashions, to the global economic crash in 2008, are intertwined throughout the text, and show how fashion responds to changes outside the sector, and aim to provide an authoritative account not only of the changing face of Burberry, but of the wider fashion retail sector.

The book is structured thematically and each chapter considers key aspects of the company which in Chapter 1 focuses on the early history of the company. We see how founder Thomas Burberry improved the position of his fledgling company through technical fabric innovation, design development and forward-looking advertising campaigns, which he used as valuable forms of intellectual property to differentiate his products from those of his competitors. He identifies and centralizes the early motorist and the gentleman soldier as key elements of his consumer base, whilst utilizing the aristocratic adventurer through what we'd now understand as celebrity endorsement and product placement.

This chapter also considers differing forms of British identity, ranging from what Buckley describes as the 'grandeur, status, and stability of British Imperial power' (2007: 33) reflected in the Classicism of Burberry's early-twentieth-century architect-designed London store, to the 'horsey' ideals of *Country Life* in the early 1950s. The importance of the aristocracy and their central role within Burberry's advertising campaigns is charted over the history of the company, showing how the company learned to generate the desire for aspiration through these key figures of wealth. Burberry's output and image analysis of their advertisements are used to explore the company's relationship to changing values within consumer culture in pre- and post-war Britain. The text also considers the impact these changes made to Burberry, and how by the late twentieth century it forced the Board of Directors to take stock of a now ailing company and appoint a new CEO to take charge of the way the company showed itself to the world.

Chapter 2 maps new CEO Rose Marie Bravo's tenure at Burberry, and examines the financial and structural difficulties faced by Burberry during this era, but also her bold ambition for the company. Burberry's problems with counterfeiting and the grey market are scrutinized and show how these were strengthened under her control. The text considers Burberry's habit of borrowing from its historic advertisements, and where in the nineteenth century the company had used real-life aristocratic adventurers, campaigns under Bravo's control show how those figures were replaced with British actors who *played* heroic historical characters in film and television, some of whom were used to promote new fragrances primarily aimed at men.

Chapter 2 also examines Burberry's move East to underpenetrated markets in China, and shows how after a long and dedicated wooing of the Chinese authorities, their loyalty and investment was rewarded. Under both Bravo and her successor Angela Ahrendts, we see how Burberry's place was secured far ahead of many other luxury fashion brands, who had only latterly attempted to negotiate with this new sector. The denouement – Burberry Beijing in 2011, heralded their new approach to fashion retail and revealed how they developed important networks and a sense of inclusion for consumers with a primarily online relationship to the brand.

Chapter 3 examines Burberry's journey before it emerged as a desirable and profitable luxury goods company with a global profile. It shows how the company calibrated and recalibrated a mix of elements, carefully balancing product, image and site alongside a distinctive choice of models – initially just Kate Moss and her polar opposite, Stella Tennant – until the distillation reached an apotheosis in a campaign released in 2005. We see how campaigns up to this time took both positive and negative turns, each unfolding in a public marketplace, impacting brand value and company profits, and what emerges from their journey is a fascinating narrative detailing an organizational and aesthetic make-over, alongside deep structural changes within the company that ultimately led Burberry to centralize a hybrid form of Britishness into its brand personality.

Chapter 3 also looks at how Burberry utilized varying dimensions of Britishness within their campaigns from 1997 onwards, using Moss as a cornerstone of the brand's British identity, showing how her profile was understood, and sometimes misinterpreted, within the United States and the UK.

Chapter 4 opens a debate about transgression and underlines how, for a short period in the early twenty-first century, Burberry became an object of ferocious criticism from fashion journalists, the financial press, consumers and even pub landlords. Bravo's attempt to widen the brand's demographic by dressing Kate Moss in a bikini and introducing lower cost and more youth-oriented products into the collection is considered in terms of class hierarchy, and assesses whether these elements also attracted working class consumers to the brand. The subsequent moral panic surrounding Burberry is examined in depth, and shows how 'bad' consumers were singled out by some sections of the UK print and broadcast media, who viewed working class consumption of Burberry as not only inappropriate, but transgressive.

Using financial press, fashion reports, UK regional and national television news, alongside unedited comments from social media, the impact of gender on public perception of the 'bad' consumer is examined, with a particular focus on how male and female consumers were viewed in utterly different ways. Conversely, we see how Burberry's links to 'chav' culture created a new anxiety in the UK, focusing in particular on what was widely viewed as excessive consumption of luxury brands and fakes. The text also highlights the contrast between 'respectable' working-class consumers, and those who were seen as undeserving, underlining how all these elements contributed to Burberry's altered state at a national level, showing how this polarized view of the company ultimately led them to be understood as a leaky brand.

Chapter 5 focuses on the closure of Burberry's production plant in Treorchy in 2007. It is described from two positions: one using distinctive labour relations and mobilization theory described in Blyton and Jenkins (2012) 'Mobilising Resistance', and from my own study, 'Can Craft Make You Happy?' (2009). Blyton and Jenkins articulate how an individualized and 'compliant' workforce were successfully banded together to take collective action to save their factory from closure, how their action went against sector norms, and how it was utterly out of character for this particular workforce. In my own study, the closure of the plant is described through oral history testimony developed with some of the women, mainly machinists, who were laid off when the plant was closed. Their words are used to highlight the deskilling in fashion production that had gone on for some time at the plant, and reveals how they reacted during and after the struggle.

The chapter also investigates the importance of place and origin in terms of Burberry production, and the text highlights a quandary faced by Burberry that as a brand asset, origin can provide what Lury (2004) argues is a guarantee of quality that is used to secure the trust of customers, whilst simultaneously limiting a company's ability to move production to take advantage of lower labour costs outside national territory. This pivotal moment in Burberry's history is aligned to a wider debate on globalized fashion production, where strenuous efforts were made by the United States and European luxury brands to retain national recognition. The chapter concludes with the launch of the £13,000 Warrior handbag in the wake of the closure at Burberry's Treorchy plant, a launch that also coincided with the height of the global economic crisis in 2008. The text investigates the wholly British line-up of models and musicians involved with the launch, and shows how these figures went some way to render opaque Burberry's increasingly slender connection with UK production.

Chapter 6 examines how international consumers were attracted to Burberry through campaigns that centralized a narrow selection of elements from the brand's history, mixed with souvenir images of London and references to England's glorious past. Analysis of their feeds on Facebook, Twitter, Pinterest and Instagram showcasing images of production plants in rural Britain and celebrated London landmarks that 'stand in' for old England, are used to show how Burberry further enhanced the heritage mythology around the brand.

Chapter 6 also analyses how Rose Marie Bravo and Angela Ahrendts approached heritage, and shows how both women used this element as a key ingredient within the rebranding process, but in very distinct ways. The text considers Bravo's fear of online platforms, which led her to concentrate on bricks and mortar stores in prestigious international locations with a long history of luxury shopping, while Ahrendts's desire to create a 'pure' brand led her to centralize digital technologies and embrace heritage through historic promotional films featuring sponsorship deals made by Burberry in the early twentieth century, which were showcased online at burberry.com, throughout its social media feeds and in its new flagship store, an Edwardian building on London's Regent Street. The chapter concludes by examining the refurbishment of this historic building by British artisans, and shows how it acted as a denouement of Ahrendts's thinking, combining digital innovation, the skill of the craftsman and luxury retail, almost mirroring Thomas Burberry's original invention-led start.

1

A one-hundred-and-fifty-year metamorphosis

In the middle of the nineteenth century, Thomas Burberry opened an unremarkable drapers store in Basingstoke, Hampshire. Burberry was a tailor's apprentice and the mainstay of his stock was a rustic cotton smock sold to local farmers and agricultural workers, but a Keeper of Art & Design at Hampshire Museum Services noted that he also sold numerous other items including fire damaged goods, trinkets and other cheaply produced products. As the company matured, Burberry expanded the women's wear and children's wear sections. Bowlby argues that at this time women, Black and immigrant groups were clustered in subordinate categories and were viewed as being easily duped, and thought 'likely to share some particularly unsophisticated (which may mean exploitable) predilections' (2000: 113), and this exploitation took place in a dualistic, hierarchical structure that favoured older, white men. The effect of the new stock and store layout meant that it was difficult for customers to compare prices on like-for-like goods and services but helped him to finesse a stronger relationship with his customers, where they responded to what Chamberlin (1933) described as irrational preferences and shopped there not by random chance, but out of choice.

The real innovation and turning point in his business came from the semi-waterproof smocks which Burberry produced in-house, and they became a catalyst for a new kind of fabric that exponentially raised his profile and the profile of the store. On hearing from a doctor that wearing clothing that used oil, rubber or wax against the inclement British weather was believed to induce ill health, Thomas Burberry collaborated with a local mill owner and successfully developed a 'weather proofed' cloth, and in 1888 he patented the new woven twill fabric as 'gabardine'. The proofed cotton fabric was woven into lengths, and was truly innovative for its time, as other companies across Britain including Mackintosh, Aquascutum and Barbour had produced 'water proofed'

Figure 1.1 Thomas Burberry's store in Church Street Basingstoke, 1910.
Image © Hampshire County Council. Image provided by Hampshire Cultural Trust.

cloth, usually as a rubberized laminate, but this was the first time that the yarn itself had been proofed prior to the weaving process, making it lightweight and breathable. Burberry's simple cotton smock had given rise to an early form of inventive production, and Burberry had succeeded in developing intellectual property features in the form of a patent for his new fabric, making the first move towards developing a non-substitutable product; the new gabardine products formed the cornerstone of the business as it was then, and continue to reflect how it performs now.

The Hampshire Cultural Trust notes that he expanded his core base of customers comprising rural agricultural workers and local people who were beginning to explore ready-to-wear clothing, to include 'gentlemen with large county estates around Hampshire who had ample leisure time for sporting pursuits'. And in 1891, the success of his new range of men's and women's weather proofed clothing meant that Burberry was able to open a shop in a London's Haymarket, and the company entered a fertile period of innovation. Thomas Burberry had succeeded in diversifying their product range through design-led features on clothing and apparel and had manoeuvred his company into a position of trust using the Burberry name as a form of guarantee, which was critical to the company as he was no longer just selling to local markets in Hampshire, but to distant buyers. The 1890s marked the birth of the motor industry in the UK, and signalled a potential new market for Burberry, as motorists needed sturdy clothing to keep out the cold and wet. In this era, many cars were open topped, so wind- and water-proof clothing became a necessity. This was a crucial turning point for his company, and clearly marked out the leisure classes as Burberry's target market.

Records at the Hampshire Cultural Trust show that Burberry supplied uniforms to army personnel during the Boer War, and this signalled another new market for Burberry's and made the military an important income stream. Burberry was developing the Tielocken, a knee-length, double breasted, belted coat, that could cope with the rigours of warfare. The originality of this design – which omitted all but a single button at the collar, and utilized a strap and buckle to fasten the coat, enabled officers to retain a well-turned-out and commanding aesthetic, the epitome of what Tynan (2011) describes as the updated military body, one that combined aspects of sporting leisurewear with new concepts of war work. On a less emblematic basis, this coat also helped officers to stay dry and warm, and differed from military-issued uniforms which were poorly made in cheap wool and added to their weight when wet or muddy. Burberry received War Office approval for the Tielocken and the 'trench' coat became a recognisable element of officer uniform. This marked an important moment for the company as it simultaneously brought two key marketing elements together: a War Office-approved officer uniform and a celebrity: Lord Kitchener was featured in an early Burberry advertisement, giving his personal endorsement to the Tielocken.

The convergence of Lord Kitchener and the Tielocken coat created a hybrid celebrity-backed product, and by meeting War Office standards for battle-ready

LORD KITCHENER

after a critical examination of other weather-proof top-coats, selected the

TIELOCKEN BURBERRY

as the most serviceable ; and has worn it during his visits to the Front.

Illustrated
Naval or
Military
Catalogue
Post Free.

*Every
Genuine
Burberry
Garment
is labelled
" Burberrys."*

N.B.—Officers wishing their Tielocken or " Burberrys" to be ABSOLUTELY WATERPROOF, regardless of hygiene, may have them interlined impervious material without extra cost.

THE TIELOCKEN

Has overlapping fronts which completely cover all vulnerable parts of the body, providing, from throat to knees, a double safeguard of inestimable value during prolonged exposure to wet or cold.

Easy Adjustment—no buttons to fasten or lose. The belt fitting the coat to any thickness of under-garments, holds it smartly and well.

Everything the Officer Needs Ready to Use
or to measure in from 2 to 4 days.

NAVAL OR MILITARY WEATHERPROOFS
Until further notice
BURBERRYS CLEAN AND RE-PROOF
Officers' " Burberrys," Tielockens and Burberry Trench-Warms
FREE OF CHARGE.
The process entails 10 clear days' possession.

BURBERRYS   Haymarket LONDON

8 & 10 Bd. Malesherbes PARIS ; & Provincial Agents.

Figure 1.2 Lord Kitchener in a Burberry 'Tielocken', 1916.
Image provided by Mary Evans Picture Library.

functionality, the company now stood for dependability and trust in the Burberry name multiplied, giving consumers two levels of accountability: the War Office and Lord Kitchener himself. Officers may well have decided that if the Tielocken was good enough for Kitchener as what he described as a 'campaigning coat', it was good enough for them. Burberry trademarked other design-led accessories including Tielocken gators, and the D-ring belt loop, which was used to attach weaponry, and this helped the company to manage future demand, by moving beyond one-off sales and establishing an identity and reputation that encouraged consumers to make repeat purchases.

Tynan's (2011) research on the production of officer-class Burberry trench coats in the First World War shows that advertisements produced by Burberry suggested that their protective clothing could create active bodies for war, and that these figures embodied the militarization of the British home front during war time. We can see through the advertisement featuring Lord Kitchener how this might operate, as in this temporal context he was emblematic of the First World War through his iconic poster 'Britons: Kitchener wants you. Join your country's army. God save the King'. Kitchener's personhood was used to attract men to sign up for military service, and as there was no conscription at this time, he played an important role on behalf of the British government. Equally, Bowlby argues that 'particularly during wartime, it was also possible to see a political role for advertising in maintaining or changing ideas of nationhood and culture' (2000: 115). We can see how Burberry attempted to manage the semiotic space around the company name, and that their approach to marketing – through invention, strong design and an endorsement from a member of the nobility, was advanced for its time. Nonetheless, Bowlby argues that the consumer still needed to be enticed over the threshold, and she writes that the 'Universal Showroom' was used to 'set the scene and get your attention' (1993: 94). Yet it took years to persuade people to break away from the idea of provisioning, where the customer entered a shop to buy essential goods, and the notion of browsing was unknown, as prior to the 1890s, 'shopping' as we now understand it did not exist. Conversely, Nava (2007) argues that the late nineteenth and early twentieth centuries witnessed a rapid change within retail, particularly the growth of urban consumer culture. Burberry's first London store did not overhaul its shop windows in order to appeal to a metropolitan elite, and it retained a utilitarian aesthetic, adhering to the retail principle of necessity, and not desire.

Advertising started to perform a distinctive role in persuading people to commit to a consumerist culture, as there were still many barriers in place – including a lack of financial resources and a lack of time, as many people spent long days at work. However, towards the close of the nineteenth century, advertising was becoming a recognized part of retail. One unlikely company revolutionized the way advertising was seen by the public, and as improbable as it sounds, this turned on an acquisition of a John Everett Millais painting by Pears Soap managing director, Thom Barrett. Barrett changed Millais' title from 'A Child's World' to 'Bubbles' and its strong connection to the business he represented transformed consumer views on advertising. McClintock argues that Barrett's intervention was especially important as it changed the axis of 'the possession' to the axis of 'the spectacle'.

> Advertising's chief contribution to modernity was the discovery that by manipulating the semiotic space around the commodity, the unconscious as a public space could also be manipulated. Barratt's great innovation was to invest huge sums of money in the creation of a visible space around the commodity. (McClintock, 1995: 213)

Though Burberry's Haymarket store retained a serviceable aesthetic, its advertisements in the press contradicted this image, as the company's fledgling marketing plan can be understood through Baudrillard's (1968) theory of sign values – where production of Burberry's officer-class uniforms went unacknowledged and hidden from view, but their consumption was strongly understood as a sign of 'gentlemanly' dress and behaviour. Kitchener's coat was not scarred with the horrors of war, but was seen and promoted as a 'campaigning' coat, with a viable use value, but one that was superseded by the image of the Gentleman Officer, greatly enhancing the semiotic space around the Burberry name, and in retrospect this period signifies a high-water mark for the company in terms of advertising and promoting its products. Records at the Burberry archive show that their preferred promotional media was to sponsor daring air flights and expeditions.

They started tentatively in 1893, supplying Burberry gaberdine to Norwegian explorer Dr Fritjof Nansen when he set sail to the Arctic Circle. Other endorsements were more visible in the public domain, including the race between explorers Roald Amundsen and Captain Scott and their attempt to reach the South Pole, which started in 1911, where Burberry supplied tents and clothing to each expedition. However, Burberry's most high-profile endorsements came from Sir Ernest Shackleton's expedition to Antarctica in 1914 and Alcock & Brown's historic transatlantic flight in 1919. This synergistic relationship – where the adventurer is generously supplied with up-to-the moment, technically innovative clothing and equipment served Burberry well,

Figure 1.3 Frank Hurley, photographer on Sir Earnest Shackleton's expedition to the Antarctic 1914, dressed in Burberry clothing.
Image provided by Getty Images (Royal Geographic Society).

and the ensuing news coverage helped them to link to widening geographic markets. This quote by Sir John Alcock now looks outdated and clunky, but at the time it was advertising gold:

> *Captain Sir John Alcock, D.S.C, the first airman to fly the Atlantic, reported as follows regarding his Burberry kit:*
>
> *'I am writing to tell you how very satisfactory the outfit has proved which I ordered for the Atlantic flight. Although in continual mist, rain or sleet, and the altitude varying from 200 to 11,000 feet causing great variations of temperature, I kept as dry as possible under such conditions.*
>
> *This was a wonderful achievement even for Burberrys, especially considering that I never adopted any electrical or other artificial means of heating, and that no rubber or cement is used in your waterproofing'.*
>
> J Alcock
Quote courtesy of the Burberry archive

At the time, Alcock and Brown were two of the most famous men in the Western world, and to persuade Alcock to talk about the brand was a coup. Burberry's proximity to adventurers and modern heroes exponentially increased their credibility and allure, which was further heightened when the company organized public exhibitions of their clothing, accessories, equipment and photographs.

From the masculine elements of Burberry's corporate sponsorships, a new and more cosmopolitan aspect of retailing was emerging in the first decade of the twentieth century – the modern department store. It was an important development within the British retail landscape, and though companies including Whiteley's, Fenwick, Debenham & Freebody, Bon Marché and Swan & Edgar had all opened stores in the nineteenth century and were trading comfortably, the opening of Selfridge's & Co. appeared rather threatening as it specifically targeted women. However, in an era when bourgeois women were dressed to communicate their husband's or father's wealth and social status, it was important to attract a female demographic to the store.

American-born retailer Gordon Selfridge opened Selfridge's & Co. in 1909, and his store featured multiple key differences including a hairdressing salon, a restaurant and tea room, customer lavatories, a library with free notepaper and a much-enhanced make up department was relocated from the basement to the ground floor, where it had previously been tucked away and regarded as somewhat shameful. Selfridges was primarily what we now regard as a destination, and not just somewhere to buy goods; the store was consciously aimed at middle- and upper-class women, however all women were welcomed into his store, including Suffragettes, and indeed one famous member of the Suffrage movement – Lady Mae Loxley, helped Selfridge to raise finance for the store when an important early backer withdrew support. Mica Nava pinpoints Selfridge's influence by recognizing the 'socio-economic and symbolic part played by women in early twentieth century modernity' (2007: 4) pointing out that Selfridge 'was a supporter of women's suffrage, advertised regularly in the feminist press and made clear his respect for the astuteness and economic power of women customers' (2007: 20). Though this gender definition looks naturalized within contemporary retail, at the time Selfridge was publicly lambasted for tempting women to spend money they didn't have – more so because it was thought to be their husband's money, as women continued to be regarded by men as highly susceptible spendthrifts, and what Bowlby (2000) refers to as pitiable dupes, easily persuaded to buy clothes, shoes and hats they didn't need. However, Selfridge built a store that was intended to accommodate women from morning until evening, and he rightly assessed the financial gains to be made by offering these amenities, as customers who could be persuaded to stay in the store for longer would inevitably spend more money.

Selfridge also introduced what we now recognize as instore experiences, including make up demonstrations and fashion shows, but a significant change to occur under Selfridge's guidance was the notion of browsing – where all goods were displayed in the open, so that customers could see what the store had to offer. This was a radical departure from the old-style department stores, where goods were tucked into drawers and cabinets and brought out singly for the customer to inspect before making a choice. Selfridge insisted that everything should be seen, and in many ways his store resembled the Great Exhibitions of the nineteenth century, where products were transformed into a series of systemized images. Nava (2008) describes how Selfridge attempted to 'aestheticise' retailing, encouraging Britain to catch up with the Americans and the French, who used window displays as part of their advertising campaigns, and not just an extension of the stock room. The huge plate glass windows at Selfridges were put to use to sell a narrative, often taking their cues from contemporary theatre and dance, where passersby became an audience, and some windows were specifically designed to be glimpsed at speed by passengers in motor cars and buses on London's Oxford Street, and this meant that the large-scale windows gave way to a new pastime of window shopping. Equally, the material characteristics of the department stores changed the experience of shopping practices; they impacted the physical environment of the modern city, and feminized what had been long been viewed as masculine spaces, as we can see from this image of Swan & Edgar on London's Regent Street from 1914.

Figure 1.4 Swan and Edgar's department store, Regent Street, 1914.
Image provided by Getty Image (Hulton Archive).

While all this excitement was going on, Thomas Burberry pressed on with his plans for expansion, and by 1913 Burberry had moved to larger premises on Haymarket. The company were now in a position to commission an architect to design the new store, and they chose Fellow of the Royal Institute of British Architects, Walter Cave, who used a Classical Revival style for the Burberry store. Buckley argues that Classicism became the dominant design approach in late-nineteenth and early-twentieth-century Britain, and Burberry's store fitted into a new imperial vision of London. 'The visual characteristics of many of these buildings were ostentation and display, achieved through a plethora of styles. Classicism was deployed to evoke the grandeur, status and stability of "British" imperial power' (Buckley, 2007: 33). The gleaming white stone exterior of Burberry's new store matched the new streets, hotels and theatres springing up in central London in this era, but in contrast to Selfridges & Co., its window displays were elegantly restrained.

Burberry retained the high-profile adventurer as a symbol of the brand, and was rivalled by Gordon Selfridge who in 1909 showcased the plane used by Louis Blériot in the historic cross-Channel flight from Calais to Dover, which

Figure 1.5 Burberry store, Haymarket London 1913 designed by Walter Cave.
Image provided by RIBA Collections.

attracted thousands of people a day to the store. However, Selfridge did not confine his events solely to the adventurer, but used his store to showcase a range of cosmopolitan interests, including the 'Russian Ballet and the Tango' (Nava, 1998: 182) and in 1914 he celebrated the store's fifth anniversary with a Merchandise of the World shopping event and special souvenir booklet, the Spirit of Modern Commerce. Selfridge's retail innovations were grounded in darker days, as the advent of the First World War loomed over Britain, but for Burberry, the war had the potential to generate significant revenue for the company.

Selling during war time

We know from the Hampshire Cultural Trust that the leisure classes were central to Burberry's success, and the First World War helped to strengthen that bond significantly. Mirroring Veblen's notion that upper class men were

Figure 1.6 Burberry officer uniform, the First World War.
Image provided by Amoret Tanner and Alamy Stock Photos.

not only exempt from industrial occupations 'but by prescriptive custom they are debarred from all industrial occupations. The range of employments open to them is rigidly defined. As on the higher plane already spoken of, these employments are government, warfare, religious observances, and sports' (1899: 4). Discounting religious observances, Burberry loyally served the three other categories.

During the First World War, men volunteered for duty and formed the mainstay of armed infantry, and these troops were led by gentlemen officers who saw warfare as their patriotic duty. However their need to distinguish themselves from the lower ranks was primarily achieved through dress, and Veblen argues that 'no line of consumption affords a more apt illustration than expenditure on dress [but expenditure on dress has this advantage over most other methods, that our apparel is always in evidence and affords an indication of our pecuniary standing to all observers at first glance]' (1899: 77). Many UK companies made huge profits in wartime, and many relied on their links to British culture: Burberry may have seen an opportunity to promote service dress in response to the inadequate clothing supplied by the Army and the RAF. Their advertising during this period emphasized speed of delivery, and the company maintained temporary outlets in France, often near theatres of war. But the adverts also drew attention to the quality of fabrics and the dependability of their officer uniforms, mirroring the success of the 'splendid Army' referred to in their 'Burberry War Kit for Officers' advert.

However, the war years were not entirely smooth for Burberry, as two years into the conflict the company was publicly scrutinized by HM Government and subjected to questions in the House of Commons. Hansard records the oral answers to questions sitting on 31 May 1916

> Mr O'Grady asked the President of the Board of Trade whether he can give information as to the extent to which Messrs. Burberry, of London, Basing-stoke, Reading, and Winchester, have in hand orders for officers' clothing either from the War Office or from individual officers; whether he is aware that the method of manufacture adopted some years ago by this firm involves the employment of women in place of skilled men, at piece rates much less than those paid in fair houses. (Hansard, 1916)

James O'Grady, MP for Leeds East, also asked the Office of Trade Boards if they had received a complaint alleging that

> Owing to the inadequate piece rates, many women work at home after workshop hours, in contravention of the Factory Act, and also whether the

firm had disregarded applications to receive a deputation of their workpeople, accompanied by trade union representatives, on the subject of their earnings, and have since, with the object of encouraging thrift, offered a special payment of 2½d a week to non-unionists. (Hansard, 1916)

Hansard records also show that O'Grady asked for an investigation into Burberry by the Office of Trade Boards in contravention to the Trade Boards Act and the Fair Wage clause, and that the results be communicated to the Contracts Department of the War Office, and to any other public departments concerned. As none of O'Grady's queries were adequately addressed by Burberry, questions continued to be raised in the House of Commons, and on 5 March 1917 William Anderson, MP for Sheffield Attercliffe, asked the Financial Secretary to the War Office whether he

was aware that at a meeting on Saturday last the cutters in the London tailoring trade decided to ballot on the question of discontinuing work in sympathy with the employés of the firm of Messrs. Burberry, at Beading (sic), whom they understand to be locked out by that firm because of their refusal to surrender their membership of the Garment Workers' Union; whether the cessation of work in the London tailoring factories would jeopardise the supply of military clothing; and whether in this case it is proposed to apply the provisions of the Munitions Act to the tailoring trade or in some other appropriate way to deal with the situation created by the recalcitrance of Messrs. Burberry? (Hansard, 1917)

The response came from John Hodge MP, Minister of Labour, who expressed regret at Burberry's lack of response to an offer of mediation, but who nonetheless sent a warning 'to the union representing the workers that any stoppage of work on Government contracts in sympathy with the employés of Messrs. Burberry's would necessarily be very seriously regarded by the Government' (Hansard, 1917). However, Hodge also stated that he had no legal power to compel Burberry to enter into arbitration as they were not manufacturing, transporting or supplying munitions under Section 3 of the Munitions of War Act 1915, but he made his feelings clear about Burberry, stating that 'I cannot help feeling that the action of the firm shows a deplorable want of that conciliatory spirit which in the general interest is so necessary in the relations between Capital and Labour, both now and after the War' (Hansard, 1917).

The ongoing battle between Burberry, the government, the skilled cutters and tailors and the employment of women shows a clear hierarchy, and one in which

Figure 1.7 Employees at Burberry's factory, Basingstoke, possibly celebrating 1918 Armistice.
Image © Hampshire County Council. Image provided by Hampshire Cultural Trust.

the female workforce found themselves on the margins, despite the intervention of several MPs supporting unionization.

After the First World War, Burberry continued to employ women and girls at industrial units in Hampshire. Employees used handcrafted production methods and we can see from the 1919 diary of Alice Attwood, a twenty-two-year-old seamstress working at Burberry, that she worked on single garments from start to finish. Attwood's cutting and sewing instructions are complex and longwinded, and made to customers' exact requirements, but she is separated from tailoring – which at the time remained strictly a man's occupation. Attwood's diary notes from Christmas 1919 show that she was making a bespoke overcoat

Navel coat regulations
Single breasted fly front
4 holes, bottom one to come 16½ inches from bottom of coat
Tab 6½ up with small buttons
Large button under lapel
Buttons to stand 3½ back
Throat tab to have 2 holes and buttoned on the inside
Facing collar to have 3 inch fall at back when finished

DB turns collar stand 1¾

Tabs on cuffs to be at angle of 40 degrees

Sleeve stitching 4 inch up

Inside tie

Pocket left facing

Pkts welts to come about 7½ inches (cut 8½)

Swing pockets with inside welt with hole and button

Outside welts 2 inches wide stitched on edge

Loose lining

Studs in cuffs, no hole in out welts

Miss A. Attwood, 24 December 1919

Courtesy of the Hampshire Cultural Trust

Burberry retained production units in Winchester, Basingstoke and Reading, and the Keeper of Art & Design at Hampshire Museum Services noted that the workforce sometimes had to chase work, cycling between each plant in order to pick up available jobs, and that the majority of female workers retired in their early twenties, where after years of working in low light conditions meant they struggled to thread a needle.

The radical changes taking place within UK consumer culture had yet to extend its reach and social change took a long time to achieve, but after the armistice of the First World War the British Government was desperate to expand the shrinking economy, and retail was gradually understood to have important economic power. Burberry had been one of the few companies to make specialist sportswear for women, and in the post-war era the company produced a range of leisure and sports apparel including clothes for golf, riding, tennis, archery and skiing. Though aimed at affluent customers, Burberry clearly understood the desires of this market segment, and produced clothing and accessories that helped to fuel the British economy. The marketing campaigns aimed at women differed markedly from those aimed at men, and we can see from this advert dating from 1925, aimed at what Burberry describe as 'the fair sex', that their use of language is significantly more adventurous and aspirational than the copy developed for men's wear advertisements. The text for this advert reads:

Switzerland! Winter Sports!

Enjoyment of which is greatly increased by wearing suitable clothing.

Burberry's, from the initiation, have specialised in winter sports clothing. Their experts have first-hand knowledge. Each year brings improvements for comfort, and brighter and more enchanting designs for the fair sex.

Snow- and wind-proof clothes in plain colours for the serious enthusiast, made in models that are thoroughly practical, with every essential considered.

There are also materials in checks and brilliant colours – many of which are really very beautiful – which have never been seen in any Winter Sports Resort.

With such clothes, new and outstanding models have been created, and the charm of these equals the beauty of the material.

There is some joy to be found in the text developed for this advertisement, and despite the feminized references to beauty and charm – terms associated with this temporal context, the excitement of a trip to Switzerland on a skiing holiday is nonetheless very alluring.

At its polar opposite, and five years after the ski advertisement appeared, we can see from a menswear advertisement in a 1930 edition of *The Graphic* newspaper, that Burberry's emphasis was still on the reliability of its products, and the illustration of The Burberry appears at odds with the Henry Heath cloche hat, and the Swan & Edgar lingerie advert. The Burberry advertising copy refers to 'drenching or continuous rain' and lists qualities including 'naturally ventilating – airtight – cool on warm days', which are unarguably good qualities in a raincoat, but which struggle to deliver any sense of excitement to the consumer, and the text ultimately refers to 'duty' – which signified burden and responsibility. In contrast, the Swan & Edgar advert is aspirational and focuses on lifestyle – their copy draws attention to the 'exquisite undergarments for the day or nightwear', and lists new and innovative easy-care fabrics including 'artificial washing satin' and 'non-ladder artificial silk'. Though these qualities might initially seem to share similarities to the robust attributes of The Burberry, there was something altogether more exciting embodied in this advert, starting with the contemporary Art Deco illustration, optimistic sunlight motif and elegant setting, but also suggestions of different ways of accessorising and styling the pyjama suit with marabou and colour contrasting trims, and a wide choice of colourways to create an inter-changeable outfit, elements which had a positive influence on consumer choice.

The period between 1920 and 1930 were challenging years for the company, and these interwar years were marked by two key factors: firstly, Thomas Burberry's sons, Arthur and Thomas, took over as joint managing directors,

Figure 1.8 Burberry specialist ski clothes, 1925.
Image provided by the Advertising Archives; all clothes and accessories by Burberry.

HENRY HEATH
105·107·109·OXFORD ST.W.

by Appointment

"VAUDEVILLE"
(Beige)
The charm of this attractive hat is enhanced by its unusual brim and loose effect. **30/-**

Obtainable from any of our Agents or sent on approval on receipt of cash or London reference.

THE BURBERRY

keeps its wearer dry and comfortable in every kind of weather.

As a WEATHERPROOF, The Burberry is "the world's best"; a safeguard that keeps out drenching or continuous rain in a truly wonderful way.

As an OVERCOAT, it is a compendium of every quality that makes for comfort when out-o'-doors.

Proof against Wet & Cold —Naturally Ventilating— Airylight—Cool on Warm Days—Warm on Chilly—

The Burberry does duty, either as Weatherproof or Overcoat, in every sort of weather, at every season of the year, and is the one coat that completely armours its wearer against every possible trick the weather can play.

"Singin' in the Rain"

Burberrys Ltd.

THE BURBERRY BOOK containing notes on the good value of the Burberry, both as a Weatherproof and as an Overcoat, patterns of materials and prices sent on mention of "THE GRAPHIC."

BURBERRYS HAYMARKET LONDON SW I

Here in the Lingerie Salon at Swan & Edgar are the most charming and exquisite undergarments for the day and nightwear. The illustrations below are typical of the good values that rule throughout this section.

Charming Negligee in floral artificial washing satin. Trimmed with rows of marabout down front and on sleeves. Finished all round girdle and pocket. In new colourings of lemon, nil, powder, peach or pink. **39/11**

Striking Three-piece Pyjama Suit in non-ladder artificial silk. Can be worn with or without coat. Trimmed with appliqués of contrasting colours. In pink, lupine, geranium, nil, lemon, black, royal or white. Sleeveless Pyjama Suit. **21/11**
Coat, 15/11   Complete, 37/-

Lingerie : Fourth Floor

SWAN & EDGAR

Swan & Edgar, Ltd., London, W.1. 'Phone : Regent 1616.

Figure 1.9 Burberry advertisement in *The Graphic*, March 1930.
Image provided by the Mary Evans Picture Library.

and secondly, in 1926, Thomas Burberry died, leaving the company without its revered figurehead and inspirational leader. However, one of Arthur and Thomas's first decisions was to copyright the Nova check design, and through this decision was perhaps one of the most crucial the company ever made, at the time this was not apparent as the check was initially used only as a pattern on a lining fabric and the weather proofed overcoat remained the dominant product. In the years after Thomas Burberry's death, the company grew more confident and started to use elements of lifestyle in their campaigns. In an advert dating from 1938, an illustration showing elegantly dressed men and women descending from an aeroplane appeared in the press. While the advertising copy still referred to the fabric, it now included references to colour, pattern, 'gossamer textures' and 'generous warmth'. Above all, it was an aspirational image of air travel, which in 1938 was still limited to the wealthy, and this seamlessly conjoined Burberry to an elite form of transport and a luxurious way of life.

However, in the lead up to the Second World War, Burberry's advertisements took on a more masculine aesthetic, which lasted for many years even after the war was over, and in the post-war period, Burberry relied on the symbolic value loaded onto the company via a Royal Warrant and their connections to the military. Changes to British retail that occurred after the Second World War, where marketing became an integral part of the design and production processes, and where the female consumer played an increasingly important role were crucial in the development of fashion retail. However, Burberry's mainstay throughout the 1940s and 1950s was the trench coat, and versions of their British Warm overcoat, and their marketing continued to reflect the company's military links, sometimes harking back to a golden age when its founder led the firm, referring directly to Thomas Burberry, as we can see from the text in a series of advertisements for the Burberry Air Warm and the Gentlemen's Walking Burberry from the 1950s.

Burberry Air Warm

The coat is based on military designs in that it carries shoulder epaulettes, wind straps on the cuffs, and convertible collar and back slit. For the trench coat and Infantry Burberry, see over.

Gentleman's Walking Burberry

This is the most popular model, being a direct descendant of Mr Thomas Burberry's (1835–1926) Original Design. Cut on classic lines, it is suitable for all occasions. It has a 'Panteen' collar, fly front, buttoning pockets and back vent

seams with a strap and button. All seams overlapped and stitched. The check
lining can be of wool, cotton or Union.

The advertising copy suggests that Burberry has moved away from a glamourous lifestyle, and there are no descriptive adjectives, simply an inventory of details. The Burberry Air Warm advertisement reinforced the company's reliance on the past, and the advert showcased an engraved image of horse riding and figures in period costume, and did not reflect an age of modernism. The company seemed to have lost the confidence they showed in the pre-war era, and when their well-heeled clients would have begun to use air travel more frequently, the company chose a horse and carriage as an element of its brand identity. In contrast to the post-war jet age, Burberry returned to conventional values.

Changes taking place within marketing in developed economies worldwide were due in part to industrialization and volume production, and in the post-war era, design for all manner of products was becoming increasingly valued by consumers. American industrial designer Harold van Doren led the vanguard, declaring that 'the job of an industrial designer is to interpret the function of useful things in terms of appeal to the eye; to endow them with beauty of form and colour; above all to create in the consumer the desire to possess' (1940: xvii). Van Doren understood that the very core of advertising as an afterthought had shifted forever, and that industrial design was a precursor to branding, where the notion of desire was starting to replace utility. In contrast to van Doren's progressive ideas about consumerism, Burberry continued to use Thomas Burberry's name in their advertising copy as a bench mark for technical excellence, and illustrations from their illustrious past that alluded to their Royal and aristocratic connections dating back to the nineteenth century. Burberry seemed to draw progressively closer to the British Monarchy throughout the 1950s, using events including the Coronation in 1953 as a basis for its advertisements, as this advert from Country Life shows.

Burberry had advertised regularly in British magazine *Country Life* from the 1920s onwards, and used what Buckley describes as a 'hybrid magazine combining news on farming, property, dogs and hunting' (2007: 69) as a basis for its outdoor wear aimed at the social elite. Burberry chose a range of themes in keeping with *Country Life*'s interests, which revolved around country sports, horse riding and the Monarchy. Burberry's advertisement shows a conservatively dressed young couple on London's Mall, directly adjacent to Buckingham Palace, and a full parade of the Queen's Horse Guards passes behind them. However,

Figure 1.10 Burberry in *Country Life* coronation special, June 1953.
Image provided by the Mary Evans Picture Library.

what makes this special for Burberry is the proximity to the young Queen Elizabeth II, which helped to create a synergistic coupling between Burberry and the Monarchy, clearly cementing the two in consumer's minds.

Where Burberry was more visibly fashionable was in editorial shoots, and this image of a Burberry houndstooth check coat appeared in Tatler in January 1959. What's striking about the photograph is its urban location, and the brutalist architecture that forms the background to this shoot contrasts sharply with the luxurious swing coat and the aristocratic aesthetic of the model. It could be argued that this image formed part of an increasingly popular sense of social realism seen in many fashion titles of the 1950s and 1960s including *Tatler, Queen* and *Harper's Bazaar,* including a Norman Parkinson fashion shoot at a Peabody Housing Estate in London in 1949 featuring Wenda Parkinson.

Burberry returned to the Royalist theme throughout the early 1960s, when for example, the British Women's Olympic team were dressed by Burberry and photographed on their way to Buckingham Palace in 1964. However, in 1968, an extraordinary set of photographs appeared in the press that matched the *Tatler* fashion editorial shoot from 1959. The setting for the photoshoot was the newly opened Hayward Gallery on London's Southbank, and this particular venue helped the company to associate itself with an absolutely up-to-the-minute element of British culture – the contemporary visual art exhibition. The pre-cast concrete structure of the building contrasted sharply with the horses and parks of Burberry's adverts in the 1950s and 60s, but the design of the collection remained conservative, reflecting a sober aesthetic seen in middle-class menswear in the UK and the United States in the late 1960s. Burberry briefly revamped its tagline *'This label is onto something new'*, and following a window display in its Paris store, where a visual merchandizer had removed the check lining from a coat and used it to create an umbrella cover, this distinctive pattern was seen for the first time as an accessory. However, this brush with the contemporary was short lived, and the company reverted to a more standard form of advertising shortly thereafter.

During the 1970s, Burberry continued to rely primarily on royal and aristocratic connections. The brand turned to Lord Lichfield as their in-house photographer, and as Lichfield was a cousin of Queen Elizabeth II, the royal connection was again vivid in the public's mind. In Britain, this link proved to be less effective as youth culture had been shaken up by anti-war protests in the late 1960s, by strikes, punk's nihilistic 'no future' mantra and high youth unemployment in the 1970s, and perhaps the country didn't much care for the sense of privilege evoked by Burberry. However, at this stage in the company's

Figure 1.11 Burberry cotton houndstooth coat, the *Tatler*, January 1959.
Photograph by Michael Molinari; image © Illustrated London News; provided by Mary Evans Picture Library.

history, exports to Japan and the United States were strong, where customers loved the historic legacy of the brand. One of the company's US adverts, featured in the New York Times in the early 1970s, used fictional character Sherlock Holmes who was depicted smoking a Meerschaum pipe, wearing a white Burberry raincoat and a deerstalker, descending from a helicopter: was this seen as a whimsical and singularly English aesthetic, and a caricature of British life? What could not be dismissed so easily however, was the company's decision to run its first Miss Burberry contest in 1970, which woefully underestimated the backlash against beauty contests, that in the same year witnessed a high-profile stage invasion by a group of second-wave feminists at the infamous Miss World pageant hosted by Bob Hope.

However, Burberry's fundamental problems were structural, as in 1955 it had become part of the Great Universal Stores (GUS) group, with label mates Wehkamp, a home shopping group, and Kay's catalogue. As time wore on, it became obvious that Burberry was the odd one out, as none of the other companies were aspirational brands, or occupied a niche position within luxury fashion.

It looked as if Burberry's management of their image, including a widespread use of licensing, where other manufacturers produced branded goods for the company, had effectively put the company into other people's hands. Many elements of their intellectual property had been handed over to manufacturers, and counterfeiting – or what Burberry referred to as 'lucrative parallel markets' (Menkes, 2002) was out of control. Burberry seemed to have all but lost their private property and had failed to nurture and protect the brand's distinctiveness, which revealed a lack of control over their trademarks, as some goods made by its suppliers were passed off as originals. The fervent grasp of post-Fordism and design-intensive work of the past seemed to be slipping through Burberry's hands, and the company seemed not to understand how it might reconnect with consumers or begin to attract new ones. The proliferation of media formats and fragmented audiences highlighted Burberry's struggle to keep up with other fashion brands, and they showed a lack of awareness of contemporary consumer culture, socialization and the consumer voice. These elements limited their opportunities to improve their public persona, and their marketing strategy proved to be linear, responsive and iterative: they kept doing the same things, and making the same things, over and over again. The 1980s and early 1990s proved difficult for many traditional British fashion companies, including Burberry's nineteenth-century contemporaries Mackintosh, Aquascutum and Barbour, all of whom produced a 'classic' trench coat and were known for their dependable outerwear. The way people consumed had changed radically over the years, with technology and marketing becoming a more central and strategic way of 'knowing' the consumer.

By 1997, further bad news lay in store for Burberry, as an article in the financial pages of the Guardian (Finch, 2000) detailed how its profits had dropped from £62 million to £25 million over the course of a single year, leading financial analysts to describe it as 'an outdated business with a fashion cachet of almost zero' (Moore and Birtwistle, 2004: 412). However, it wasn't just the critiques delivered by financial analysts that dogged the company – it was also failing to attract new customers. How would Burberry fight back and revive its fortunes?

Conclusions

This chapter highlights the important role of founder Thomas Burberry as he is what Lury describes as a 'live person standing behind the brand' (2004: 80), with an ability to add value to his company, highlighting the loss of this 'lone genius' when he died. We see a side to Thomas Burberry that is rarely discussed – his collaboration with another textile professional, where he worked in partnership with a local mill owner to develop an innovative and high-tech cloth. This proved to be one of the company's most enduring and profitable legacies, and one that helped to create the foundation for Burberry's early success. It also assisted the company to define and develop its core customer base – the military officer, the motorist and the sportsman, and was an astonishingly successful partnership, but one that has never been repeated.

I've attempted to show how both the First World War and the Second World War assisted the company to build considerable revenues by targeting gentleman officers, and how this also shaped the brand in the post-war era. We also glimpse a hard-line stance against its own workforce during the First World War, where union negotiations faced the unmoveable and staunchly capitalist position of the company, even attracting the attention of central government in Westminster.

This chapter highlights how London's West End became a more feminized space after Selfridge's & Co. opened in the first decade of the twentieth century, and despite developing and retailing clothes for women, Burberry's new store on London's Haymarket retained a pared back, masculine aesthetic that was closer in style to its Jermyn Street neighbours, famous as a destination for men's tailoring, shoes, hats and guns. Although Selfridge's innovations were bold and cosmopolitan, his success was still some way off as he was seen, like the women in his store, as an outsider in British society.

We also start to understand Burberry's complicated relationship with the Great Universal Stores group in the mid-1950s, and how this profoundly altered the way the Burberry was seen as it was structurally aligned with low-value, mundane companies that shared none of the aspirational qualities more usually linked to a luxury fashion brand.

In the next chapter, we see the appointment of a new CEO at Burberry in 1997, who attempted to realign and reinvigorate the company. The chapter also examines the impact of a slowly diminishing manufacturing industry in Britain and the United States, and we see how this is replaced by the service sector, where fashion retail plays an important role.

2

A new rose

In late 1997, Burberry made a surprising new appointment when it announced that Rose Marie Bravo was to be their new CEO. Bravo emerged from a career in retail at Saks Fifth Avenue and Macy's, and bought a new kind of energy to the company: she saw huge potential for the firm, but that came not from the design of new collections, but in how they were marketed. This clear change in direction signalled a new style of leadership and a new direction for the company, and Bravo came out fighting, uttering these unforgettable words shortly after her appointment was made public 'the goal is to turn the Burberry name into a brand as hip as Gucci, Louis Vuitton, or Prada'. (encyclopedia.com). At this time, Burberry's values as a company represented a view of Britain as what *New York Times* journalist Suzy Menkes (2002) described as 'horsey, classic, snobby and dowdy', and it could be argued that their relationship to identity, culture, status and class was the very antithesis of the kind of optimistic images consumers now sought. And while her statement aligning Burberry with three high-profile luxury brands was bold, it also looked unfeasible.

At this time, Burberry did not produce goods that reflected contemporary knowledge of consumer tastes, habits or preferences, only serviceable ones that were functional and resembled its military past, as if identity was still likely to be defined by rank. McCracken (1988) argues that designed and branded goods are *given* meanings before they get to the consumer, and as Menkes (2002) makes clear, the sign values around Burberry were largely uninspiring to those who fell outside the 'horsey' set. Burberry's lack of appeal can also be understood through Hebdige and Willis (1982) who argued that consumption can be seen as a political form of expression against bourgeois taste, and as Burberry was widely viewed as an embodiment of a bourgeois lifestyle – and indeed the company had spent many years creating a space around the brand that firmly connected the company to the bourgeoisie, it is understandable that Burberry was not particularly attractive to consumers in contemporary culture.

However, 1998 was a transitional time for the UK, and a New Labour government had recently been voted into power and were anxious to sweep in an era of modernization, and make London the capital of cool. But at this time Burberry was far from a representation of Cool Britannia, and the company needed strong leadership to take it into the new century. Anticipation surrounding Bravo's lead mounted, and as Menkes pointed out in a retrospective editorial on the new CEO's appointment 'it took someone from outside the British class system to understand the value of the company', and that Thomas Burberry

> the visionary who founded the company in 1880 and made his raincoats a service to the military and sporting worlds – had become a prophet without honor in his own county. Despised by the British [Burberry had become linked to a group of people as narrow as its product focus]. (Menkes, 2002)

One of Bravo's first acts was to bring the vast majority of licensing back in house, spending millions of dollars bringing raincoats, umbrellas, scarves, sunglasses and gloves back into their control, helping to ensure high-quality products. Bravo worked to strengthen Burberry's legal position to ensure that its hard-won private property was returned to them, and remained in their hands. Burberry pursued all counterfeiters, retaining relentless and total control over their property, and against anyone 'passing off' their products, thereby protecting the brand's distinctiveness.

One of the key products under a licencing agreement were their fragrances, and the company selected British actor Hugh Dancy to front the Burberry Brit campaign, who at this time had become synonymous with his role as young British hero in the BBC television production of Daniel Deronda (2002). Dancy went on to play Galahad in a film production of King Arthur in 2004, and the Earl of Essex in the 2005 television series Elizabeth I, further cementing his profile as a heroic and aristocratic Englishman. It was clear from these decisions that Bravo was working hard to update Burberry, particularly through its marketing campaigns, and the company invested heavily in British models including Dancy, and subsequently with actor Ioan Gruffudd, who fronted the Burberry London fragrance campaign. Like Dancy, Gruffudd was also linked to a heroic, historic fictional character, Horatio Hornblower, appearing in the titular role on British television in 2003.

This image of Dancy in the Burberry Brit campaign can be situated within a resurgence of men's interest in fashion and grooming from the mid-1980s onwards.

Figure 2.1 Hugh Dancy for Burberry Brit, 2003.
Photograph © Mario Testino. Image provided by Art Partner New York; all clothes and accessories by Burberry.

We can see that Dancy is dressed in a two-piece suit, a white shirt and dark tie, all of which are standard items of men's wear, however this image separates him from a mainstream aesthetic, as Craik (1993) notes that within dominant culture, men predominantly dress for comfort and not style, and those who are interested in fashion may be viewed as 'peculiar'. However, Dancy looks relaxed and stylish and far from Craik's proposition of peculiar; his longish hair is groomed, as is his facial stubble, and his hands and nails are clean and manicured. His suit is what Tim Edwards would describe as a 'uniform of respectability' (2011: 43) and is made from a luxurious fabric, but his tie is loosened which gives a sign of informality to his appearance. The luxury sports car he leans against makes the whole image aspirational, and removes any assertion of being what Edwards describes as 'not masculine' (2011: 42), and closer to what was commonly understood as the 'new man'. Frank Mort (1996) describes how as a result of the rise of the new man, the homosocial gaze shared between heterosexual men are fixed on mutual displays of admiration, and it is easy to see how Dancy might be admired by men for his stylish looks and adventuring on-screen persona.

We can situate Dancy's image and the product itself within a growing attraction to male grooming within mainstream culture, which was reflected in the expanding market of men's style magazines including *GQ*, *Arena* and *The Face*. However, Burberry Brit was sold widely in high street stores in the UK including Superdrug and Boots, and was, like many fragrances from luxury brands, a significant revenue stream for the company. But where Burberry were selective in their choices for press campaigns for their clothing lines, which were limited to prestige fashion titles only, their fragrance campaigns were sited on billboards in *JC Decaux* and *Adshel* sites across many urban areas including working-class communities. Could Dancy's perceived upper-class image as an Oxford graduate, privately educated at a 600-year-old English public school be at odds with working-class consumption of this elite brand?

'Hornblower' actor Ioan Gruffudd fronted the Burberry London fragrance campaign, paired with another British actor, Rachel Weisz. Gruffudd had appeared alongside Dancy in the King Arthur film production, where he played Lancelot, and these adaptations of classic British historical narratives were sufficiently high profile to reach an international audience. While most consumers would have no knowledge of the real aristocrats and adventurers used by Burberry to endorse their products in the early years of the company, nonetheless a strong and vivid link to this romantic and heroic way of life was forged through these television and film adaptations that linked the brand to historical adventures and derring-do of a particularly British type.

Dancy's Burberry Brit campaign was tightly controlled and aspirational, however the Burberry London campaign stood in stark contrast, and the selected aesthetic was a series of scrapbook images of Weisz and Gruffudd. For Burberry London, photographer Mario Testino followed the pair to a classic phone box, then to London landmarks including the London Eye, Big Ben and the

South Bank, all high-profile tourist destinations. The image was edged in Nova Check, the pack shot was prominent, and overall, the advert linked Burberry to romance, picturesque scenery and quaint London streets. Quite by chance Weisz won an Academy Award *for The Constant Gardener* (2005) during her contract with Burberry, and her status as Cambridge graduate coupled with her profile in Hollywood, where she was known as a true English beauty further enhanced the brand. Quite simply, Burberry could not have bought the additional attention and kudos that her Oscar brought to the company, as it combined beauty, wit and intelligence and seemed to sum up all that was glorious about both the British and the brand in the key North American market.

Another significant milestone of the early 2000s was the redevelopment of the Burberry Prorsum line, and though it was, and remained until its dissolution in 2016, a small collection, it proved important as it enabled the company to show at Milan Fashion Week, and gave them invaluable and positive coverage for the first time in decades. In 1998, Bravo initially appointed Italian designer and textile expert Riccardo Menichetti to work on the Prorsum line. Menichetti had worked at French fashion house Claude Montana and at Hamburg-based Jil Sander, developing designs for both companies, and perhaps Bravo imagined he could bring some of Thomas Burberry's magic as a craftsman back to the company, however his tenure as head designer was short lived, and in 2002 Royal College of Art women's wear design graduate Christopher Bailey was appointed as design director. Bailey had worked at Donna Karan and with Tom Ford at Gucci as a junior designer; he was well versed with working for North American fashion companies, and understood where Bravo was leading the company.

At that time the role of chief designer at Burberry was not as high profile as it was to become over his sixteen-year tenure. However, Bailey's public utterances on clothes, style and music were useful to Burberry, and he proved to be of value as someone who could help to extend the brand. Bailey quickly became Chief Creative Officer, and an essential part of the Burberry experience and the company's economy. His story of working-class origin was familiar to readers of *Vogue, Elle, The Times, The Telegraph* and a plethora of upmarket print media and online fashion titles, and his biography made Bailey into the living embodiment of the meritocratic ideals of the Burberry brand. Bailey's personhood was useful in troubled times, and he became the familiar, friendly and benign face of the company, who was regularly called upon to calm situations, for example in the moral panic that followed Kate Moss's exposure as 'cocaine Kate' in autumn 2005. Burberry appeared in an editorial in *British Vogue*, perhaps in an attempt to counteract public anxiety, and journalist Justine Picardie was dispatched to interview Bailey, accompanied by regular Burberry model Stella Tennant. Moss was nowhere in sight. 'Burberry told its creative director Christopher Bailey to follow his heart and he did just that, finding inspiration in his own Yorkshire roots. Vogue takes him back to his home county with local girl Stella Tennant' (Picardie, 2006: 175–9). The interview and photoshoot took place at Bolton Priory, land owned for centuries by Tennant's family via William Cavendish, the seventh Duke of Devonshire. The rural setting and the addition of the aristocratic model allowed Burberry to paint a picture that reassured consumers that Burberry was not the place for drug busts or squalid lifestyles. The setting for the photoshoot allowed Burberry to utilize what Corner and Harvey (1991) argue is the mythology of social order, where the country house captures the serenity of long-established families and a harmonious relationship between people and the environment. In the same interview Bailey delivers a perfect soundbite for the company:

> Did you know that the company has a factory in Yorkshire, near Wakefield, where we make the Burberry gabardine trench coats? And we still use fabrics from the traditional local mills. I love those solid English cloths, they're so durable, they have a solidity and functionality about them. They are really designed to last, which is why you'll hear people in the mills talking about a heavy tweed, tough enough to withstand thorns and thistles. (2006: 175–6)

Bailey fills our imagination with images of bucolic beauty, honest labour and long-lasting functionality, but he also uses the region to feed a nationalist agenda about goods produced in England, building an unrealistic image that leads us to believe that Burberry produces all its goods in idyllic rural settings. This was used to increase the brands' desirability but it also allowed Burberry to levy premium prices for products 'designed to last'. Bailey continued to be used to deepen consumer relationship with the brand, and he is credited with overseeing every aspect of design at Burberry, including all fashion ranges, accessories, fragrance and make up, runway shows, advertising campaigns and the new headquarters on Horseferry Road in London. However, he is also used to present a real person to the public, serving a similar role as Tom Ford at Gucci, and in many ways Bailey resembles Wally Olins's (1978) vision of the corporate personality, where image and reality cannot be detached. His role at Burberry became multifaceted, for example in addition to his design work he is also credited with overseeing Burberry Acoustic, an in-house initiative where young UK-based musicians were showcased on the main website and on Burberry's YouTube and Vimeo channels. Burberry used Bailey's role to insert him into what Arvidsson (2006) describes as networks of communication – he can recreate social occasions and outings, witness his 'date' with Stella Tennant on her family's private estate.

After nearly ten years in the post, Bravo retired and in 2006 Angela Ahrendts stepped in as the new CEO. Ahrendts shared a similar background and educational history to Bravo, with qualifications in merchandising and marketing followed by a role as President of Donna Karen International, and subsequently as Executive Vice President at Liz Claiborne. 2006 was a critical year for Burberry as it marked their 150th year in business, and the anniversary campaigns under Ahrendts seemed to emphasize Burberry's links to noble British ancestry and new hip connections, and she selected a line-up of youthful actors and musicians, and the offspring of some well-known British figures including Richard Branson, David Bailey and Bryan Ferry.

An image of Otis and Isaac Ferry, Stella Tennant and Kate Moss formed a key part of the anniversary campaign, but this line up can be interpreted in different ways, sending mixed messages to consumers. For example, Otis Ferry, elder son of Roxy Music's Bryan Ferry, is infamous for his pro-fox-hunting views and had been arrested by the police on numerous occasions: in August 2002, when he was nineteen years old, he was arrested while attempting to plaster stickers over Tony Blair's constituency home in County Durham when the government planned to introduce a bill to prohibit hunting with dogs. He is also famous for storming the Houses of Parliament in a pro-hunt protest, and in 2006 he was prosecuted for drunk driving. Subsequently, in 2007, as Master of the South Shropshire Hunt, Otis Ferry was remanded to Gloucester prison, charged with witness intimidation, robbery, assault and perverting the course of justice, and was later found guilty of a public order offence. Otis's brother, Isaac Ferry, is also no stranger to controversy, sending this email to an anti-hunt campaigner in 2002, prompting his expulsion from Eton. 'You are a fucking looser (*sic*). Why don't you stop waisting (*sic*) your time and get a real job/hobby, you cunt' (wildlifeguardian.co.uk; Wildlife Guardian).

Burberry may have hoped to send a message about family, Britishness and tradition, yet the image can be read as evoking privilege and entitlement. However, Burberry framed these choices through the adoption of what Arvidsson (2006) describes as putting the aristocracy to work – using its connections to the nobility through their selection of models, for example Stella Tennant is the granddaughter of the Duke and Duchess of Devonshire, and Otis and Isaac Ferry's mother, formerly Lucy Helmore, was, until her death in 2018, Lady Birley. Where Burberry once used aristocratic adventurers – Lord Kitchener, Sir John Alcock and Sir Earnest Shackleton, and learned to work aspiration through these key figures of wealth, placing the utmost importance on traditional prosperity, and not new money, there is a clear line through the history of the company linking 'tastemakers' who are mixed with well-heeled but hip socialites including Cara and Poppy Delevingne, granddaughters of Sir Jocelyn Stevens – formerly the head of English Heritage, with Sting's daughter, Coco Sumner; the Ferry family continued to be represented through Tara Ferry, who was paired with Annie Lennox's daughter, Tali. These images present a rich seam of stability and reassurance that in a time of economic uncertainty proved to be a very valuable signifier.

By 2009, Burberry was financially successful and globally visible, however what is rarely discussed, and is not evident from their advertising images, is the design of the main collections. At first glance, this seems like a huge oversight by the company, however as Lash and Urry (1994) argue, ordinary manufacturing has been superseded by the production of culture and a more generic symbolic-processing capacity. Consumers are aware of Burberry, but as Lash and Urry suggest, they are using their symbolic-processing capacity to assess not just the design of the clothes, but the entire brand, where consumers – but not working-class consumers, are not limited to a single sector, but are free to consume across multiple sectors.

The move East

We see the production of consumer culture writ large in Burberry's Chinese market, and it is often credited as a key element in the financial success of the company. Burberry used Bravo's tenure very effectively as she frequently travelled there for business, often staying for extended periods of time, and because of the company's perceived devotion to China, Burberry were welcomed by the new authorities and established strong links within their emerging economy long before many other brands had even started to develop markets in the Far East. Ahrendts capitalized on Bravo's connections, and moved forward with plans to develop new retail outlets in multiple cities, including flagship stores in Beijing and Shanghai, rapidly swelling Burberry's customer base in the Far East. The highlight of Burberry's relationship with China came in 2011, when they opened their Beijing store and hosted a holographic runway show at the Beijing Television Sound Stage, with 900 carefully selected guests. This was a significant time in Burberry's history, and cemented the company's importance as a luxury brand within Asian markets.

Figure 2.2 Burberry Beijing, 2011.
Photograph by Ian Gavan. Image provided by Getty Images; all clothes and accessories by Burberry.

Burberry Beijing was created as a massive cultural production, utilizing music, film, fashion, visual art, holographic 'magic', satellite technology and live streaming. A huge team, comprising Government officers from the UK Trade and Industry office, The British Ambassador to China, Burberry management, designers, service sections, including technical, retail and catering staff, along with indie band Keane. Each stage of the production was carefully choreographed, and an overriding statement – repeated by Ahrendts, Bailey and Tom Chaplin, lead singer of Keane, as the financial section of *The Telegraph* reported 'Beijing is not dissimilar to London, and to Burberry. China is a very old country, but with a young dynamic culture and the future of Burberry and the future of China are inseparable' (Hall, 2011). Images from the event showed that everything was branded with the Burberry Nova check – from the trucks feeding the satellite links, the bars serving drinks, staff uniforms, to the floodlight entrances. Iconic images of London's Big Ben, were beamed to a worldwide audience, and the event became a total immersive experience for invited guests and online viewers alike.

Although Burberry was in the process of expanding their bricks and mortar retail presence in China and in other international markets, they understood that an increasing number of customers had an entirely online relationship with the brand, which changed the way they interacted and consumed. While

Burberry had not committed entirely to interactivity or new media saturation, it had developed two important online elements to their brand, Art of the Trench and Runway to Reality. Runway to Reality was a live streaming service featuring their London Fashion Week runway show, that started with their Autumn–Winter 2010 collection. Burberry developed proprietary digital technologies that meant individual customers could watch the show from the comfort of their home, and order clothes, shoes and accessories directly from the show without waiting for them to arrive at their local store. Runway to Reality proved to be a huge success with consumers, as it gave customers from all over the world direct access to what was once a privileged, A-list-only invitation to an exclusive show at London Fashion Week, which very few people saw live. Though I wouldn't argue that the runway show is what Lash (2002) would describe as an 'old media' presentation, it's true to say that it demands attention – if briefly – and it's site specific, you have to travel to see it; though the clothing collections are new, the *form* of the show comes from something old, and in that sense it is detached from everyday life. Burberry's developments profoundly altered the relationship between consumer and retailer, as they packaged the excitement of the live show (even using a digital clock on the Burberry site counting down the days and hours before the live runway show at Fashion Weeks in February and September) whilst online guests could see front row celebrities and feel part of the event. Huge digital maps detailed where the show was beamed to, giving a sense of international inclusion, and customers could circumvent the long delivery time, and order in their size and colour choice before it was sold out.

The upside for Burberry, in addition to the increase in sales that followed, came from data mining going on behind the scenes, which gave them invaluable information on their customers, but it also gave them what Arvidsson (2006) describes as an investment in consumer involvement, where brand management was an active process, and gave Burberry a chance to pre-structure consumer activity into their desired directions. Burberry's preference was a sinking-into-the-background approach over interactivity, data mining over consumer activity and recommendation rather than what Lury (2004) describes as talking back. They also use what Lash (2002) describes as media-comes-to-the-consumer campaigns, and never opt for a more interactive approach, such as pop-up online adverts, street promotions or any other ambient forms of marketing. It was understandable that Burberry would want to protect their value and retain their status as a luxury fashion brand, however the downside of this led to what appeared to be emotionally clingy behaviour, where the brand wants the consumer to 'like us on Facebook', or 'follow us on Twitter', but perhaps they felt the cost of consumer criticism was too great. Where we might have expected the company to be a little more relaxed was on the Art of the Trench fan-site, where members of the public were invited to send in photographs of themselves dressed in a Burberry trench coat, but there too was a rigid control over what and who appeared. Art of the Trench was not an obscure section of their website – it featured alongside all the major parts of the company, but it was not the democratic area it appeared to be, as a forceful but soundless creative control gave the online images an over-arching generic quality, and gave consumers no opportunity to engage with or 'talk back' to the brand.

Despite the development of some important digital platforms, Burberry continued to increase their stores on a global basis, and the opening of their London flagship store on Regent Street in 2012 formed an important element of the brand. The development of this store was a key achievement for Ahrendts as she expanded Bravo's initiative to make it the most important channel to attract new customers, and used it as a partner – with the website – to attract customers to the store. Ahrendts understood that developing the store into a destination point and centre for immersive retail experience was vital in contemporary shopping, and she is quoted on Vogue.com saying that

'Burberry Regent Street brings our digital world to life in a physical space for the first time, where customers can experience every facet of the brand through immersive multimedia content exactly as they do online', said Burberry CEO Angela Ahrendts.

'Walking through the doors is just like walking into our website. It is Burberry World Live.' (Alexander, 2012)

Burberry had succeeded in creating a fully immersive, entirely branded environment that allowed customers to experience the clothes, the sounds and the history in a Burberry-fragranced atmosphere. The site of the building was crucial – London's Regent Street is arguably more accessible than their Bond Street store, yet it retains the history of its royal past. Their Bond Street store nestles next to art and antique shops, fine jewellers and the London flagship stores for Chanel, Dior and Louis Vuitton, which can be intimidating spaces to some shoppers. I made a site visit to the Regent Street store shortly after it opened, dressing carefully in my newest clothes and a pair of high-heeled platform shoes and was silently checked by the security men at the front door. Entering the store I was greeted with a magnificent interior expensively clad in blonde stone and blonde carpet, with a double height projection screen at the rear of the store, featuring a rolling programme of images that included archive footage of the Nova Check weaving process, sepia-toned photographs of men at cutting tables, motivational messages including '121 Regent Street: seamlessly blending the physical and digital worlds' and 'Burberry: a celebration of British design and craftsmanship'. Older links to adventurers and explorers were also represented on screen, alongside stars from Burberry Acoustic in what the brand described as a digitally-enabled cultural space.

Burberry had a long lead time to develop its retail environments into gallery spaces, and the Regent Street store delivered their vision unreservedly. Each of the three floors was experiential, starting on the ground floor with the more price-accessible Burberry collections, rising to the Burberry Bespoke and Prorsum lines on the top floor minstrel gallery space, which blended a mix of browsing with more contemporary ideas about interactivity, including reactive mirrors showing catwalk images and touch-screen displays for customer use. The sum of these parts leads to what Arvidsson (2006) describes as a controlled context in which consumption takes place, where the store acts as a frame for the brand. Many aspects of the store hark back to earlier times, and some – like the mirror finishes, emerge from the dawn of advertising and resemble what McClintock describes as an exhibition aesthetic: a display of commodities within a polished environment, free of the imprint of human hands and labour. Burberry uses mirrored surfaces at its liminal aspects in order to tempt consumers over the threshold, and to lure them 'deeper and deeper into consumerism' (McClintock, 1995: 218). But this too expresses a contradiction as the highly polished exterior, free of dirt and fingerprints, exerts what McClintock argues is an erasure of the signs of labour, and turns the mirror into the epitome of commodity fetishism, and a controlled border between public and private. It is strange to think that these ideas are far from new, and far from innovative, yet strangely compelling. The Regent Street store is, as Ahrendts suggests, the living embodiment of their website, but more than that, it is a reflection of the company and its ethical, financial and intellectual principles.

Conclusions

During Bravo's time at Burberry, she successfully brought the brand into the public consciousness, and certainly some of her decisions were well thought through and strategic, including her attempt to halt mass counterfeiting by buying back licenses from 1997 onwards. Burberry were successful in stopping companies who should have been making legitimate goods for the company, but who were flooding the market with cheap reproductions. What additionally stood out was that Burberry went after third party hosts, including payment processors PayPal Inc., winning the right to intercept monies generated from sales. Sponsored search engines including Google, and social media platforms including Facebook and Twitter were legally prevented from doing any future business with any defendants who had been prosecuted for counterfeiting, and can now be held accountable for associating with the sites.

Bravo's astute eye for marketing was evident in the increase in fragrance sales to men. By understanding the importance of male grooming in this era, and expanding the network of stores to include high street retailers and a wide-reaching billboard campaign, Bravo was able to strengthen sales for the brand by selling not just to elite consumers, but to working class men. This posed a paradox for Burberry, as around this time, the brand was increasingly linked to the 'wrong' consumers, which begs the question: was this the start of the mini-moral panic surrounding Burberry in the mid-2000s?

One of the key success stories is Burberry's foray into digital platforms, and in their Regent Street flagship store Ahrendts made a facsimile of their online site, creating an immersive environment around the brand. The Regent Street store successfully synthesizes both leisure and consumption, but it also serves as a site of interaction and co-creativity with consumers through online initiatives including Runway to Reality and Burberry Acoustic, both of which were spectacularly successful. Equally, the role of the Regency building is rooted in brand communication, and the building's architecture is used to deliver an external relationship with the environment, leading to what Jansen-Verbeke argues is a 'strong assumption that the historic setting is a major point of attraction which adds considerably to the appreciation of a leisure environment' (1990: 135). Ahrendts's desire to create Burberry World Live as a homogenous 'pure' brand, offering the same product offer and store design had become a reality.

In the next chapter, I show how this pure brand was momentarily disrupted by examining Kate Moss's role within Burberry, and how as a working-class model who fronted the company in the early days of Bravo's re-branding campaign, her personhood may have sent mixed messages to working-class consumers, particularly those based in the UK. I also examine the way Burberry expresses Britishness through their choice of models and through the development of its marketing, showing how it delivers sometimes contradictory results in the UK and elsewhere in the world.

3

Surviving through Britishness

In 2005, an image of Kate Moss dressed in a classic stone-coloured trench coat appeared in the national and international fashion press. The image formed part of Burberry's Autumn–Winter global marketing campaign, and the advert appeared in worldwide editions of mainstream fashion magazines including *Vogue*, *Elle*, *Harper's Bazaar*, *InStyle* and *Marie Claire*, each with a large readership in countries as diverse as Japan, Russia, India, China, Mexico and Australia, as well as European, North American and Scandinavian markets. The advert signalled a sea change for Burberry, and served as an emblem marking a successful transformation from clothing company to an internationally recognized luxury fashion brand.

The advert contained three important elements – an elegant mews, a cobbled road and a black cab – all of which played significant roles in building a strong semiotic image around Burberry, optimizing its geographic ties to England and specifically to 'heritage' London. These particular elements were important as they gave shape and form to an historic and valuable backdrop for the emerging brand, however I'd argue that the addition of Moss fundamentally disrupts the image and adds a contradictory element, specifically in the UK, as her working-class status runs counter to the image of a company known for its strong links to elite consumers, and takes the image in a radically different direction. The addition of Moss as a central character in Burberry's rehabilitation further complicated what Lash (2002) describes as their representation, as she is simultaneously a symbol of Cool Britannia and what Angela Buttolph (2008) described as a global style icon, but also an authentic working class woman. How did Burberry find itself in this moment, and what propelled them to choose Moss?

Figure 3.1 Kate Moss for Burberry, Autumn–Winter 2005.
Photograph © Mario Testino. Image provided by Art Partner New York; all clothes and accessories by Burberry.

Burberry reborn

Rose Marie Bravo's appointment at Burberry in 1997 can be viewed alongside an era of government-endorsed privatization, a long-running and saturated programme started under Margaret Thatcher's Conservative government that came to fruition in the 1990s. The initiative involved the privatization of a range of large-scale public companies including British Airways, British Gas and British Telecom, who subsequently required a new corporate identity in order to mark the distinction between government control and their new status as private companies listed on the London Stock Exchange. Concurrently, many companies started to examine the economic effectiveness of working solely with advertising agencies, particularly in relation to expanding media platforms and fragmented audiences, areas in which the agencies had limited capabilities. Liz Moor defines how during the early 1990s 'a diffuse set of practices – product design, retail design, point-of-purchase marketing among others – became consolidated into an integrated approach to marketing and business strategy known as branding' (2007: 3). Moor describes how multiple branding consultancies were formed during this era, often taking work away from the old advertising agencies, as they were able to offer a broad vision and a total communication package and not simply an advertising campaign. This new integrated approach provided Burberry with an economic rationale to cope with changes in retail and consumer behaviour, and a clear framework to relaunch their business. 1997 was a turbulent year in British politics that saw a seismic change in leadership as New Labour won a landslide victory, ending an eighteen-year Conservative rule. The Conservatives' plan to establish London as a global financial centre was well underway, but it was New Labour who made financial history, as after only four days in office the new Chancellor of the Exchequer, Gordon Brown, announced that the Bank of England was to assume independent responsibility for monetary policy including setting UK interest rates. Perhaps these specific political and economic conditions gave Burberry and Bravo a sign that this was the right time for change?

In the early to mid-1990s, Burberry worked with Christy Turlington – one of the first global supermodels, on a series of adverts that shared visual parallels with some of the most sought-after designers in the United States, including Calvin Klein and Ralph Lauren. However, these campaigns also shared an aesthetic with emerging brand J Crew, which had been a mail order catalogue and in-home demonstration company, Popular Merchandise, until it changed its name in 1983. J Crew focused on leisurewear for upper-middle-class consumers, and sought to emulate a Ralph Lauren aesthetic, but at a much lower price. In Britain, some of Burberry's UK marketing in 1997 shared aesthetic values with clothing company Next, who – like J Crew – aimed to produce high quality designs at a lower price point. However Next used high profile British model Yasmin le Bon in many of their campaigns, and successfully elevated the sense of aspiration for many customers. In terms of silhouette and colour palette, there were similarities between Burberry and Next, but also styles featured in the Spring–Summer 1997 mail order catalogue Kay's of Worcester. Burberry adverts from 1997 show beautifully lit images that exude warmth through the choice of colour and tint, however the clothing and accessories – even with the addition of important trademarks like the Nova check and the Equestrian Knight logo – link Burberry with mid-market fashions from Next, which had become an aspirational label for middle-class consumers, and to mail-order catalogues including Kay's, which was primarily aimed at low-income families. Had a lack of differentiation between Burberry and product from other women's wear brands caused the company to become entangled with a price range at the middle and lower end of the fashion market? What had led Burberry down this path, far away from the high-quality fashion and apparel sector at this point in its history?

The Great Universal Stores (GUS) group acquired Burberry in the mid-1950s, which was seen as an unpredictable move as GUS were primarily known for their mail order businesses including John England and Kay's of Worcester. GUS had expertise in mail order retail and specialized in furniture and household goods, but lacked experience within the luxury fashion sector and, despite being part of the group for over forty years, Burberry did not enjoy any high visibility recognition and its image was further subsumed into the GUS business strategy, which targeted customers with a lack of access to credit. This set the tone across the group, and painted an image of a corporation whose profits were primarily made through weekly payment instalments. The disparity between Burberry and its parent company made a classic form of information asymmetry as the association between a volume market, mail-order business aimed at working-class consumers, impacted the up-market company. In retrospect, retail analysts including Nick Hawkins from Merrill Lynch pointed out 'and of course Burberry is not truly a core business for GUS' (Heller, 2000a). It seemed clear that Burberry was an orphan within the giant GUS conglomerate, and in 1996 modifications to the GUS Board of Directors saw some rapid changes made by the new Chairman of the group, David Wolfson. He presided over a change in leadership at Burberry, but bad news lay in store for the new Chair, as in early 1997 the financial press reported a sudden drop in profit at Burberry, caused principally by the financial crisis in Asian and Japanese markets. Forbes Global reported 'by the mid-1990s the Far East accounted for an unbalanced 75% of Burberry's sales' (Heller, 2000b).

The economic crisis impacted export trading across Asian markets, but Burberry's over-reliance on this customer base hit the company hard. An article in Forbes from January 2000 (Heller, 2000b) details the predicament that Burberry, and GUS, found themselves in, and it suggests that the Board of Directors clearly understood the value of the Burberry brand name, making it financially un-worthwhile to sell it off. Burberry Chairman Victor Barnett told Forbes

> The truth is we could never get the real economic value out of the company by selling it. Because Burberry has such a large upside opportunity, and we really understand where we're going, we think we can do better with shareholder value by doing the job ourselves. (Heller, 2000b)

What made Burberry decide to hire a new CEO, and more specifically what made them depart from their customary pattern and hire externally and not from someone already within the group? Following a business model put in place at struggling luxury corporations Louis Vuitton Moet Hennessy (LVMH) and the Gucci Group dating from the early 1990s, Burberry recruited Rose Marie Bravo, perhaps hoping to emulate Tom Ford's success at Gucci in 1994. But there was a crucial difference between Ford and Bravo – Ford joined Gucci as Creative Director and was an experienced designer, whereas Bravo's experience was in marketing. Barnett clarified GUS's motives for Bravo's appointment

> 'Repositioning Burberry requires dealing with a great many specifics and that takes time', says Barnett. 'This is one reason why Rose Marie is so good for us, because at the crux of the business is the merchandising and marketing, the creation of revenue.' (Heller, 2000b)

Barnett clearly pinpoints the epicentre of the rebranding exercise and clarifies the reason for appointing a marketing expert, and not a designer. Bravo started work at Burberry in late 1997, and though working with reduced revenues, one of her first appointments was New York-based branding consultancy Baron & Baron who worked with her to develop the 'underexploited [name recognition value]' (Heller, 2000b) at Burberry. Baron & Baron, like many of the newly formed branding consultancies offered 'a full spectrum resource able to conceptualise and produce consistent communications across virtually every platform' (Baron-Baron.com). Baron & Baron's aim was to support Burberry to 'actively strategize and manage each aspect of the company's growth and development, [helping them to anticipate and successfully navigate ever changing global trends, shifting markets, and consumer tastes]' (Baron-Baron.com).

Bravo's aim at the outset of her tenure was to make Burberry as hip as Gucci, Louis Vuitton and Prada, and in 1997 the brands that Bravo sought to emulate were already using sophisticated visual language through their marketing campaigns which helped them to establish innovative profiles and a wider consumer base. Baron & Baron had worked successfully with Prada for a number of years, and the consultancy had also helped to shape campaigns for Dunhill and Pringle, two clothing companies with origins in other centuries, which gave them experience in repositioning brands with considerable but not always desirable histories, and this made them a good fit to fulfil Bravo's aims.

Campaign images from Gucci, Prada and Vuitton differed radically from those at Burberry, and all three brands experimented with differing forms of fashioned identity. Some images borrowed from fine art, for example a Prada

Spring–Summer 1997 campaign shot by Glen Luchford, resembled the pre-Raphaelite painting Ophelia by John Everett Millais dating from the mid-nineteenth century. Vuitton worked with photographers Inez and Vinoodh and some of their images from 1997 used elements of camp and questioned gender norms. Gucci commissioned photographer Mario Testino to shoot their campaigns, and images from their Autumn–Winter 1997 shoot tested the limits of sexual identity.

One of the first images to be published under Bravo's control featured model Stella Tennant, who was photographed by a close associate of Baron & Baron, Mario Testino. Bravo used the rebranding programme to move the company towards what Moor (2007) describes as countering existing perceptions of the brand, which in this instance were what Barton and Pratley (2004) described as 'fusty and fading', however some aspects of fade were recontextualized in this image, including the misty, monochrome tint that gently underlines the historic nature of Burberry. Similarly, Testino's image makes use of the unmade path, dry-stone walls and rocky outcrop, connecting the brand to an ancient rural landscape, which gives an impression of an enduring and cyclical natural world that Corner and Harvey (1991) argue makes for a timeless past of social history and hallowed custom. Tennant plays the role of a parent picking up a child from school, and though she has her back to the camera, her high-heeled, sling-back shoes are clearly visible in the frame, and indicate a hip and privileged lifestyle, and not an agricultural one. Burberry has cleverly used what Moor (2007) describes as a transformation of abstract values – of the rural and ancient coupled with the chic, into a material form, one that inspires aspiration and carefully sums up the essence of the brand. The image shows how Bravo had started to construct a highly specific representation of 'Britishness' through her international marketing eye, and working alongside a consultancy led by the French-born Fabien Baron, it becomes clear that they were capable of delivering a uniquely hybrid version of Britishness aimed at the global market.

This was an important image for Burberry as they attempted to distance the company from its recent lacklustre past, and it becomes clear through this campaign that they had embraced a new fashion aesthetic forged by two emerging creative forces, photographer Corinne Day and stylist Isabella Blow. Though independent of one another, their work for magazines including *The Face* and *Dazed & Confused* in the early 1990s marked a clear shift away from the glossy fashion images emanating from North America, and a move towards a less conventional style of beauty. Burberry's campaign mirrored a new grunge aesthetic and the campaign was seen as identifiably British. The 1998

Figure 3.2 Stella Tennant for Burberry, Portmeirion 1998.
Photograph © Mario Testino. Image provided by Art Partner New York; all clothes and accessories by Burberry.

image featuring Stella Tennant began to set a pattern for future marketing campaigns, where a combination of elements including the British countryside, a monochrome colour palette and the use of British models provided a distinctive backdrop to the emerging brand, however Burberry changed direction for their next campaign as perhaps the lack of visibly recognizable Burberry trademarks, or even the windswept and bleak countryside may have proved too oblique for international markets.

In 1999, Burberry came back with an image featuring British model Kate Moss. The advert was published in the United States and the image used more of the distinctive Nova check pattern than the 1998 campaign, making use of this important trademark in an attempt to raise the company's visibility within the valuable North American market. The background image was a more manicured outdoor aesthetic, where a dog with a velvety coat, a tree-lined horizon and a cut lawn created a more manageable sense of the rural than the 1998 campaign. Burberry's reasons for casting Moss in the central role may have been because she was already well known in the United States through her advertising work for Calvin Klein in the early 1990s. This, coupled with her romantic connection to actor Johnny Depp, had exponentially increased international press interest in her, and allowed Burberry to use her proximity to Hollywood 'royalty' to maximum effect.

However, the image started to expose a fault line between brand perception in the United States and in Britain, where at this time Moss was strongly identified as the face of heroin chic, but equally as a girl from Croydon, which at this time was a predominantly working-class suburb on the outskirts of London and 'the second most miserable place to live in the UK' (Huggins, 2013). Moss told *The New York Times* that during the early days of her career ' "I thought I'll do whatever it takes," Ms Moss said with a laugh. "Anything to get out of Croydon" ' (Trebay, 2012). The derogatory term 'Croydon facelift' – which describes hair pulled back into a tight ponytail, resembling extreme cosmetic surgery, was a pejorative slur used against working-class women and girls, and in Britain Moss became entangled with the term. In 2004, online bulletin board 'BB Fans: UK Big Brother Forums' described how Moss was positioned alongside glamour model Katie Price and Big Brother contestant Michelle Bass – celebrities known for their Croydon Facelift look. However, both Price and Bass were relatively unknown outside the UK, especially in the important US and Asian markets, which gave this narrative a singularly localized British class focus, indicating that international consumers were untroubled with any downsides to Moss's profile. Yet in the UK, as Burberry's rebranding programme relied on social, political and economic factors, using Moss complicated their corporate communication and identity, as she was not what Pilditch (1970) describes as an adjunct of their advertising; she was at the core of the brand.

In 2000, Burberry again swapped Moss for Stella Tennant in the central role, moving the company away from a working-class context, at least in the UK, as the photoshoot took place in Wales – a radically different site to the urban working-class environs of Croydon.

The site of the campaign positively influenced consumer perception, and what Kellner (1993) describes as our interpretation of the image added a wistful and romantic element to the brand. Tennant, who is the daughter of the Honourable Tessa Tennant, and great granddaughter to the Duke and Duchess of Devonshire, helped Burberry to exploit links between the company and a genuine 'blue blood' in order to increase brand value, in the same way as they did with Lord Kitchener and the adventuring aristocrats in the early years of the twentieth century. The new Burberry, under Bravo's control, had returned to a long-standing British tradition of using titled women as models, and started to re-lay a foundation showing the brand's proximity to the British aristocracy, however Bravo understood that the company couldn't simply return to the past, they needed to mix it with something cool and stylish in order to connect with contemporary consumers, and Tennant helped Burberry to fulfil the brief. At the outset of her modelling career, she was cast in *British Vogue*'s seminal portfolio shoot 'Anglo Saxon Attitude' (December 1993) and through this editorial she became known as the 'aristo-punk' as her pierced septum and angular features fell outside classic model aesthetics, but she possessed what *British Vogue* described as looks and lineage. Anglo Saxon Attitude was styled by Isabella Blow, and shot by American photographer Steven Meisel, and he understood Tennant's intrinsic value, calling her a patrician vision of Britain.

The image for the 2000 campaign shows Tennant and a child straddling her shoulders in relaxed and informal poses, and it appears to be utterly contemporary, however a closer inspection reveals signposts to the past, including a tiny silhouette of a horse and rider on the horizon, which not only harks back to company adverts from the 1950s, where Burberry used facsimiles of nineteenth-century engravings as a way of referring to their illustrious history, but which also draw an image of what Goodrum describes as 'a version of Britishness in which good taste and cultural-economic rank are inherited, also revolves around a code of exclusivity and exclusion' (2005: 131). So, the pony and rider are not in a public space, they occupy private property, and the consumer is permitted only a glimpse into this exclusive environment

Figure 3.3 Stella Tennant for Burberry, Wales 2000.
Photograph © Mario Testino. Image provided by Art Partner New York; all clothes and accessories by Burberry.

from which they are otherwise excluded. The issue of inheritance is key to this image, and Burberry have used birthright as a way of extending the brand, selectively mixing elements of aristocratic history and modern life, then re-presenting it in a contemporary way using what Lash (2002) describes as

Figure 3.4 Kate Moss for Burberry, Spring–Summer London 2001.
Photograph © Mario Testino. Image provided by Art Partner New York; all clothes and accessories by Burberry.

an old media format – the magazine advertisement, to hint at a long duration of British values.

This image of patrician British life proved to be particularly valuable in the United States where the 2000 campaign was successful in terms of US media profile, attracting bi-coastal editorial coverage in the North American press, (Bellafante, 2000; Herman-Cohen, 2001) but Burberry nonetheless changed direction again, and published this image featuring Kate Moss and an ensemble cast of players.

This campaign included renowned and high-profile models Naomi Campbell, Jerry Hall and Marie Helvin; however, it was this 'shoplifting' scene that proved memorable. This extraordinary image – polar opposite to the cool, aristocratic setting of the previous campaign, shows a different side to British life, and exudes a wealth of visual cues ranging from the glossy Euro-style of Moss's male companion, to the beady eye under the 'Madchester' bucket hat pulled down over the eyebrows. After Moss, the Madchester character has the most central role in this tableau: he looks tense, and his eye is in constant surveillance of the things and people around him, however the scene also looks familiar to him, and his practiced hand is used as a signal and a cover for the theft perpetrated by a well-heeled woman, who stuffs what appears to be unpaid for clothing into a branded carrier bag. Moss looks directly into the photographer's lens as her companion pays for the shopping, distracting the Sikh sales assistant as the theft takes place. She looks insouciantly at the viewer, and though her role in this advert is 'the girlfriend', her gaze towards us shows that she is clearly in charge of this scenario. The cultural diversity, age range, and social status of the characters in the advert is broad, however the overall image veers towards the comedic, showing a side of British culture that trades on a pantomime-esque Carry On-style imagery, representing what Tanya Gold (2008) describes as a 'cartoonish mirror to the depressed and repressed Britain of the 1950s and 1960s' and effectively returns Burberry to a working class context. There are opposing elements at play throughout the image, including a distinct lack of respectability as the theft seems condoned by us, the onlookers, and we are invited to collude with the characters and the action, ultimately hoping that Moss and her co-conspirators get away with the theft.

Moss appears to be invested in the action, and though we understand very little about her at a local level, in a British context she is perceived as both an international star and a wilful working-class woman. This interpretation of Moss is supported by this image where she portrays a character on the edge of lawlessness, and is seen to inhabit what Skeggs describes as a 'body beyond governance' (2005: 965). Moreover, the comedic nature of the advertisement, where Moss seen to be 'having a laugh' is a strategy that Skeggs argues is a way of 'staging resistance to authority' (2005: 975) that in this instance is the theft of high-cost clothing from a luxury retailer. By fronting the brand, does Moss signify a call to arms for working class consumers to choose Burberry? This faced the company with a dilemma: how could the brand use Moss's working-class status without making the working classes target consumers? The same campaign included images of Moss and Naomi Campbell spilling out of a nightclub, and Jerry Hall and Marie Helvin play-fighting over a pair of branded shoes, and in Britain these acts of public misdemeanour had a significant down side for some consumers, and could not be read coherently. In Britain, this campaign took the brand in an undetermined direction, and though Burberry aimed to position itself within the luxury market, its meaning became diffused as the brands' connection to working class life positioned it in a less positive way, however in international markets, the connection between Burberry and the supermodels signified only high quality.

Had Bravo's career in the United States dressing 'perfectly groomed women of all ages but one income tax bracket' (Herman-Cohen, 2001) narrowed her eye for what constituted Britishness? Undoubtedly, there seems to be a lack of nuance towards British national identity, and an underestimation of how this image would impact on working class consumers in the UK, but perhaps Bravo was chasing cool from a US perspective?

America the Brave in British class war

Certainly, Bravo's real strength was her embodied knowledge of the North American luxury fashion retail market, where she had worked for over twenty years and which was key to Burberry's international expansion. Her intimate understanding of that sector indicated that the focus of her sales and marketing was in the United States. Bravo was correct in her assumption that the 2001 campaign would be popular in the United States, where reportage was positive and viewed as charming and entertaining. The *Los Angeles Times* described them as 'whimsical ad campaigns created by photographer Mario Testino and art director Fabien Baron' (Herman-Cohen, 2001).

Throughout this campaign, we see how Burberry's brand intangibles became polarized and highly context specific, as market segments in Britain and the United States reacted in wholly different ways. For example, in the UK, the increase in working-class consumption was met with an escalation of increasingly panic-stricken press headlines, especially those barring entry to pubs and clubs for anyone wearing Burberry, while in the United States, wealthier consumers turned to the 'plucky Brit – Burberry' (Herman-Cohen, 2001) which systematically impacted brand reputation and level of consumer trust, resulting in an upturn in sales. In May 2001, Bravo's carefully planned market research included a lunch at a restaurant in Beverly Hills 'filled with 24 of the most influential and powerful women in Los Angeles' (Herman-Cohen, 2001).

> A charming Burberry plaid tote swung from the arm of Kelly Chapman Meyer, wife of Universal Studios chief Ron Meyer, while Lauren King of the King World Productions empire mixed her vintage ivory Burberry coat and trousers with Hermes accessories. (Herman-Cohen, 2001)

This snapshot draws a strong image of a handful of privileged women wearing Burberry to a specially organized lunch, and demonstrates how the company had started to successfully rebrand itself to a narrow but key demographic in the North American market. However, a new flagship store on a corner of Wilshire Boulevard, launched in September 2001, not only widened the market, but was material evidence of that success. The *Los Angeles Times* reported that 'as the 19th U.S. store, it will be a smaller version of the London flagship on Bond Street, larger than South Coast Plaza's, and in many ways, more important than both' (Herman-Cohen, May 2001). Though the Wilshire Boulevard store was vital to the rebrand, its importance relied heavily on its British connections – Burberry's history, its links to the aristocracy and the very fabric of its famous trench coats and Nova check lining – however the article in the *Los Angeles Times* shows how the British market had become marginal, and for the first time in the rebranding programme there is a palpable sense of a split between what Heller (2000) describes as 'the old brand and the new look'. Perhaps the British market was just too small to be significant, however Burberry looked as if it might be promoting less-than-abundant information for customers, and had created a fundamental change within the company: it was not just bringing goods to the market, it was actively shaping a new market.

Bravo's management background at Saks and I. Magnin stores suggests that she was very comfortable with her role as the 'pacesetter of high-profile society' (Goodwin, 1989) but she seemed to struggle to connect to a wider consumer base, despite her well-publicized desire to make Burberry more accessible. She told the *Los Angeles Times* in May 2001 'we're not about a certain arrogance or elitism', Bravo said. 'We're trying a more democratic approach. We have an internal tag line', she said, 'Burberry at any age' (Herman-Cohen, 2001). By 2001, Burberry had introduced more product lines to appeal to a wider age group, and their retail offer now included the Nova check bikini, headscarf and baseball cap, but had the company neglected to think how these products might be used by working-class consumers in the UK? When Burberry employed faux-Madchester imagery in the 2001 campaign, coupled with Moss in a central role, did the overall aesthetic appeal more widely to working-class consumers in the UK? Certainly, the contrast in imagery between the up-scale consumers in Los Angeles's Wiltshire Boulevard and Manchester in the late 1980s couldn't have been more polarized.

Though separated by more than half a decade, there is a slip and slide with the meaning of Madchester and its relationship to the more temperate and government-endorsed Cool Britannia that followed. Bravo and brand consultants Baron & Baron could not have failed to notice the media attention

Cool Britannia attracted in the United States – a Newsweek cover from November 1996 declared 'London Rules' and the magazine ran an editorial on 'Inside the World's Coolest City'. In March 1997, *Vanity Fair* published a 'Cool Britannia Special' where Liam Gallagher, the stylish Oasis singer and his wife, actor Patsy Kensit, were featured on the cover under the title 'London Swings Again', wrapped in a Union flag. Cool Britannia was well received in the United States, and this may have foregrounded Bravo's decision to go ahead with imagery alluding to the Madchester/Cool Britannia sub-cultures, using Moss as a central element in the campaign, as by the mid-1990s she was strongly identified with Cool Britannia through her connection to Oasis – she had played tambourine on two tracks from the seminal Definitely Maybe (1994) and Be Here Now (1997) and appeared live on stage with the band in an acoustic set at the Virgin Megastore in London in 1994. Cool Britannia had been largely neutered by the deadening hand of political approval, nonetheless Oasis emerged as the rebellious face of the movement, as Cosmo Landesman observed 'then there was a group of young and dynamic creatives who became associated with Cool Britannia, like those bad boys from Oasis, the Gallagher brothers' (2009: 257). Cool Britannia gave the UK a momentary sense of self-belief, and the era was seen as a new Swinging Sixties, celebrating music, fashion and culture. It formed part of New Labour's intent to re-brand Britain as Cool Britannia using Tony Blair's description of the UK as 'a people and society characterised by know-how, creativity, risk-taking, and most of all, originality' (Bevir, 2005: 47). Like Moss, Noel and Liam Gallagher came from a working-class background and wholly embodied these characteristics; they were the classic freelance, creative entrepreneurs that Blair and New Labour wanted to celebrate. Moss and the Gallagher brothers had grown up in an age of Thatcherism, and though lacking educational and cultural capital, they more than made up for this with an abundance of 'know-how, creativity, risk-taking and originality', which maximized their economic capital to the hilt. Burberry recognized and used what Polly Vernon (2006) described as Moss's potent image currency and positioned her in the central role, but did not acknowledge any deep-rooted class distinction.

Burberry were more effective in channelling the positivity that Cool Britannia brought to the UK and built on it to strengthen brand value by emphasizing their connection to Britain, so when in 2004 the European Commission proposed to launch a Made in EU label as a way of competing with the Made in the USA mega-label, they were proactive in the protection of the brands' origin and its value to the company, and fought hard to retain their Made in Britain status.

Online intellectual property specialists IPKat reported on the media campaign orchestrated by luxury brand lobbyists the Walpole Group.

> Businesses in several EU Member States are unhappy about this, since they want consumers to know where the goods they buy are actually coming from – particularly those companies that emphasise their national ties and trade on their Britishness (like Burberry) or Scottishness (like Scotch whisky). (IPKat, 2004)

Burberry, in collaboration with Walpole, worked with EU members in France and Italy and together they publicly distanced themselves from other European countries including Portugal, Poland and Turkey, stigmatizing them as lacking in craftsmanship, tradition and expertise. Burberry returned to the crux of their business – merchandising, marketing and the creation of revenue, through a reaffirmation of their Britishness. This involved maximizing what Pike (2010) describes as the geographical entanglements deeply embedded in their intellectual property, and for Burberry the relationship between branding and IP was especially important in relation to their increasingly busy international trade, but this was primarily achieved through their marketing images and not in the manufacturing, sourcing or employment sectors of the company.

The Autumn–Winter 2004 campaign strengthened Burberry's geographical links to Britain, and specifically to London, with a campaign shot in Spitalfields, formerly a traditional East End market adjacent to another souvenir attraction, Petticoat Lane. This image featured Moss and a Pearly King and Queen, and references 'pearly' life, a hospitable and charitable tradition of white working-class custom stemming from the nineteenth century. Burberry's 2004 collection was based mainly around the trench coat presented in a variety of colourways, which in campaign images was relegated to a narrow border, utterly marginalized by the flamboyance of the Pearly King and Queen (who in real life were music hall act Larry Barnes, aka 'The Viceroy of Versatility', and his stage assistant Maggie). Moss's aesthetic in this image is restrained and unrecognizable as Burberry, comprising a black, cropped trouser suit, ankle-length sock, court shoe, and a white shirt. But what this image communicated is a sense of companionship between Moss and the 'pearlies' that endorses this very particular aspect of urban London life to the global consumer. The marketplace adds a public, sociable element to the setting that is far removed from the abstract and complex market that Burberry operates within. This was an astute move by Burberry as the image of an historic figure like the Pearly King and Queen is an unusual facet of British culture and one that would intrigue international consumers, and for those who recognized the largely well-loved characters, it signified a

Figure 3.5 Kate Moss for Burberry, Autumn–Winter 2004.
Photograph © Mario Testino, Image provided by Art Partner New York; all clothes and accessories by Burberry.

joyful roll-out-the-barrel knees-up around the piano, and an authentic slice of British working-class culture.

The image of the East End Pearly King can also be read as a sign of whiteness, which went against the cultural diversity of the area – a predominantly Bengali neighbourhood, and a community who are notably absent in the Burberry campaign. Wemyss argues that the 'white pearly king remains at the top of the social hierarchy as the "guv'nor"' (2009: 111) but only at a local level, and Watts (2007) argues that pearly culture was increasingly viewed as retrogressive, even within their own families, who felt a sense of embarrassment about the tradition. However, as this advert formed part of Burberry's global marketing campaign, the Spitalfields site played an important role in placing the brand in a context that highlighted the cosmopolitan breadth of British culture. For example, the doorways seen at the back of the shot are old Huguenot weavers' cottages dating from the seventeenth century, which placed the brand in a context of an ancient artisanal expertise, and at this time the area was also home to artists Gilbert & George, and to writer Jeanette Winterson's café and deli, Verde, which gave it a contemporary cosmopolitanism and individuality and successfully rendered the site as an important but quirky tourist venue.

Despite their marginal status in the marketing campaign, Burberry's Autumn–Winter collection was a commercial success, and the 'new ranges of more colourful designs have also proved popular with shoppers, [in Europe, the United States and Asia] including a pink version of its classic raincoat' (BBC News, 2004a). Bravo and brand consultants Baron & Baron had found a successful way of communicating a sense of international Britishness into Burberry's brand values through Moss and the pearlies that successfully communicated *we're down to earth and fun to be with,* and indeed this sense of fun was carried into other marketing campaigns from this era.

A model of Britishness

Burberry marketed a strong sense of Britishness through their choice of models, using young women that *British Vogue* described as 'confident, individual and quirky'. British ex-pat Victoria 'Plum' Sykes, contributing editor at *American Vogue*, argued that 'A model who is funny is commercial (And we Brits are famously funny: sarcasm and self-deprecation are as much part of our cultural make-up as HP sauce and bad weather)' (Fox, 2014: 192). A sense of fun is centralized in Moss, and knowing how to have fun is one of the key characteristics of her public identity, and fundamental to how she is perceived in both the UK and the United States. However, in the UK, Moss's profile as a committed carouser is strongly linked to her social class, for example when Bez (dancer with Madchester band Happy Monday's) befriended Moss in the early 1990s, he declared 'she's a proper working-class girl, and she knows how to have fun' (Time Out, 2006) but her sense of fun was intertwined with something entirely more risky, an element of which was reflected in Burberry's Spring–Summer 2004 campaign. The marketing images captured a narrative of a hedonistic lifestyle in a setting that resembled Ibiza, and featured Moss and Theodora Richards, daughter of Rolling Stones guitarist, Keith Richards. Ibiza's reputation as a party island with a long connection to drug culture created a backdrop for a collection of paint-splashed clothing that suggested an idyllic, indolent, everlasting holiday. In the campaign, Moss wears a huge pair of sunglasses in the early morning summer haze, which can be read as an attempt to cover up after a heavy night of revelry. However Moss's authentic party-hard lifestyle strongly mirrored her role in the 2004 campaign, and though recreational drug use is not uncommon in the modelling community, Moss was set apart from the mainstream as she was profoundly unapologetic about any out-of-control behaviour and was widely viewed as an 'unrepentant party girl' (Trebay, 2012). However, the connection to Ibiza's long history of drug culture can also be read as information asymmetry that distorted Burberry's market, and the question then becomes – does a holiday on the island inevitably lead to bad behaviour under the guise of having fun? And did the gaps and incomplete information presented by Burberry cause their more conventional consumers to be fearful through association, not only with Moss, but through connections visited in Keith Richards's daughter?

On this occasion, Burberry's Spring–Summer 2004 campaign was strangely prescient, as just over a year later Moss was photographed by the *Daily Mirror* snorting cocaine in a London recording studio. Bravo took immediate action and sacked Moss on the spot, as her rebellious lifestyle – though valuable when it was under control, had perhaps become too close for comfort and threatened to impact the brand. The drug allegations came in the same year as the successful denouement of the 'new' Burberry and the company's triumphant passage into the global luxury market, and the image of Moss in a London mews, conservatively dressed in a trench coat, court shoes and a sensible handbag earlier in 2005 contrasted badly to the press shots of her in September that year. A spokesperson for Burberry issued a statement saying that 'Ms Moss was scheduled to participate in a campaign this fall, but "both Kate and Burberry have mutually agreed that it is inappropriate to go ahead"' (Dodd, 2005). In Britain, after the cocaine scandal in 2005, Moss was portrayed as the antithesis of a hygienic, cleansed image of white Britishness, and Burberry's dilemma was how to extricate the brand smoothly from the drama, however corporate strength quickly overshadowed Moss's own fight back, and the brand rapidly issued a statement wishing her well (Dodd, 2005) and in the public domain at least, they were seen as a caring company. This perception differed from a scenario suggested by Eric Wilson in *The New York Times* (2005) who pointed out that perhaps the real reason for Burberry's concern wasn't an act of brand benevolence, but hard finance, as it may have been just too expensive to pull the campaign at such a late date. Ultimately, Moss suffered the same fate as any other white working-class woman who got out of line, and quite simply she was forced to display what was widely perceived as a lack of moral values on a global platform. For over seven years, Moss had helped to immeasurably increase Burberry's profitability, and we also know that her addition was widely credited as 'the most significant factor in the brand's renaissance' (Vernon, 2006), and while her dismissal was only temporary, she was let go as it was seen that she could actively damage brand value.

Conclusions

This chapter highlights the differences and contradictions in dimensions of Burberry's Britishness in the UK and in the United States that shows a split between the British as traditional and patrician, whilst simultaneously party-loving and cool. We saw how the driving forces behind Burberry's rebrand, Bravo and Baron & Baron, constructed a form of Britishness that both played on and ignored class values, using Tennant to embody the aristocratic, and Moss as a wild card – elements that were viewed in a positive light in the United States, but which signalled an uneasy amalgam of sartorial elegance and working-class intervention in the UK. Suzy Menkes, writing in *The New York Times* reported on this UK–US split

> It took someone from outside the British class system to use eccentricity and wit to bring back Burberry's legendary status in its own land. Seeing Kate Moss, London model turned international star, in a redesigned Burberry trench coat was the 'click' that gave Bravo the sense of how to mix a legacy of credibility with hip, young street cred. (Menkes, 2002)

Menkes underlines the crucial role that Moss played in the rebranding of Burberry, and as a British journalist based in the United States since 1988, she was in a strong position to understand the role of the UK class system from within the United States, and to see how the brand fared on their shores. Menkes also highlights the importance of eccentricity and wit as another critical factor in Burberry's US success, and we saw from an article in the *Los Angeles Times* (Herman-Cohen, 2001) that 'whimsy' became an important and newsworthy element, and that Bravo attempted to tie this quaint form of humour to the brand.

In 1997, Burberry embraced a post-Thatcherite creative identity that *British Vogue* described as an 'iconoclastic creativity Britain does best' (Fox, 2014: 191) and Burberry's reemergence in the 1990s coincided with a significant but unconventional aesthetic which marked a clear shift away from the glossy supermodels exemplified by North Americans, Linda Evangelista, Christy Turlington, Cindy Crawford and others, and a move towards a less conventional type of beauty that was seen as inextricably linked to Britain. This grunge aesthetic was wholly embodied by Moss and Tennant and both models became the unofficial British figureheads of the new look, as Moss's short stature and uneven teeth, and Tennant's pierced septum and androgynous features departed from classic model appearances. Their value to the company was the role they played in the new cohort of models who typified 'Britishness' as a place 'where tradition and anarchy sit side by side' (Fox, 2014: 191) which helped Burberry to move the brand away from its mid-market, conservative past and bind it to an image of Britain where the capitalistic sheen was removed from the previous decade's fashion.

Burberry's rebranding programme coincided with the dismantling of large sections of government-owned industries that relied on the term British – Telecom, Airways etc. – as a way of identifying their origins, and as denationalization attempted to shrink the state, other more inventive ways of declaring geographic roots took their place, which at Burberry ranged from a pony and rider on a private estate, ancient rural landscapes, Pearly Kings, to Madchester and Cool Britannia, providing an indelible stamp of 'old Britain' mixed with cool youth subcultures.

Burberry reflected the drift from the local to the global by conjuring a sense of nationhood through its marketing campaigns, largely fulfilling Colley's (1999) sense of Britain as an 'asymmetrical, composite state full of different but inchoate allegiances'. This helped Burberry to construct a sense of place that not only made room for idiosyncratic campaigns, but actively encouraged eccentricity as a selling point. However, despite the move from the local to the global, the 'Made in the EU' campaign showed that Burberry were determined to boost brand value through the company's origins, and by collaborating with France and Italy to strengthen their association with what Aaker (2000) describes as perceived quality, they allied themselves to countries with highly visible couture traditions.

The enormous changes at Burberry between 1997 and 2005, reflected a wider debate in the mid-1990s about a declining sense of nationalism and the growing importance of globalization. Billig (1995) argued that the processes of globalization resulted in a diminished difference and fragmented what he describes as an imagined unity within nations, and Burberry formed an almost perfect microcosm of this state through their increasingly standardized, internationally available collections, but also through Moss and Tennant, who represented polar opposites of what international consumers thought typified 'British'. We learn that by chasing a nationalistic dream, Burberry effectively harnessed the aspirations of a new generation of international consumers, but find that they were attracted to what Billig (1995) termed a quiet nationalism – a non-extremist, everyday 'banal' nationalism – that Burberry used as a framework for centralizing Britishness and making it significant in a contemporary, global market.

Skey (2011) asks if national identities matter and, if so, to whom? Perhaps in Burberry's case, the answer is that they matter more to individuals living outside the nation state, as the brand sells the idea of Britishness as an idealized discourse within a global market. Indeed, Interbrand's annual survey for 2006 named Burberry as the 'most successful commercial export of "Britishness" to date' (Sweney, 2007) indicating that the path chosen by Bravo and her successor Angela Ahrendts was a strong one that pushed the brand in to ever more profitable areas.

In the next chapter the wider implications of Bravo's decision widen the product range at Burberry is examined, asking if the inclusion of lower-cost and more fashionable items including a bandana and a bikini helped to attract a working-class consumer demographic to the brand. The chapter also focusses on the issue of 'good' and 'bad' consumers within the UK market, and asks if this can be further subdivided by gender.

4

Good and bad consumers:
The lost fight and the fight back

In 2000, to coincide with Burberry CEO Rose Marie Bravo's decision to introduce lower-cost product lines into the mainstream collection, the company published an image of Kate Moss wearing a Nova check bikini and white bridal veil. The image is casual – the characters are laughing and chatting together, the action takes place in a domestic kitchen and overall, the image borrows from a home photo aesthetic. Skeggs points out in her work on 'reality' television that creating a believable '*mise-en-scène* which makes use of familiar settings such as kitchens, gardens, living rooms, etc.' (2008: 562) creates a relationship with the viewer that helps us to perceive that what we are seeing is 'real', and that vivid sense of realism is evident in this image. The overall aesthetic is low-key, behind-the-scenes and accessible, and the props – a bouquet and a veil, are used to reproduce a facsimile of a hen party showing the women preparing for the night ahead. For many UK consumers, it is a joyful scenario as the hen party forms a precursor to one of the best days of their lives, but for others it is the subject of moral disgrace as it alludes to what Skeggs describes as 'loud, white, excessive, drunk, fat, vulgar, disgusting, hen-partying woman' (2005: 965). The scene sets up a contrasting sense of affect – on one side it leads to what Ahmed (2004) refers to as the pre-determined happiness of the wedding day, and in the opposing corner the image embodies what Skeggs describes as 'the moral obsession historically associated with the working class' (2005: 965) which in this case is the out-of-control woman having fun at a hen party.

Burberry has a long association with working-class culture, from its beginnings as a supplier of hardy outdoor wear for agricultural workers in the mid-nineteenth century, and when it was structurally embedded in a mail-order retail sector that was primarily aimed at working-class consumers. But mail-order shopping also gave less well-off consumers a sense of pride as they found a fiscally responsible way of paying for luxury goods, and consequently these

Figure 4.1 Kate Moss and Liberty Ross for Burberry, Spring–Summer 2000. Photograph © Mario Testino. Image provided by Art Partner New York; all clothes and accessories by Burberry.

consumers did not see themselves as 'bad' for buying Burberry, nor did they acknowledge any transgression of invisible dress codes by buying the brand. Up to the early years of the twenty-first century, Kay's catalogue sold Burberry clothes and accessories through weekly payment instalments, and it remained a point of pride to customers and employees alike that Kay's was the only catalogue in the UK to offer Burberry. In an audio clip on the University of Worcester's worldofkays.org (© University of Worcester) research project, former Kay's employee Anne Thomas reflects that the large customer base was 'slightly higher class than competitors since, unlike them, it included Burberry and other high-value brands' (worldofkays.org, 2011).

In the fifty years after the Second World War, mail-order shopping in the UK was given a radical overhaul as it distanced itself from the low-quality, low-grade aesthetic of the pre-war years. Kay's became part of the Great Universal Stores (GUS) conglomerate in 1937, when the pre-war association with home shopping was what Joseph Fattorini, owner of the Empire Stores mail-order business, termed low-class trade. However, by the time Burberry was acquired by GUS in

1955 there was a feeling of respectability connected to catalogue shopping, and Coopey, O'Connell and Porter argue that 'working class consumers in the post-war era, however, expected better quality – the wartime Utility Scheme had made an important contribution to this respect' (2005: 61). Two key factors helped to enhance the sector: the stringent quality control measures put in place by individual companies, coupled with the introduction of branded goods. Branded goods had the potential to excite consumer appetite for mail-order, as the public already had confidence in the products, but this was not a straightforward move for the mail-order companies and Coopey and others observe that there were

> Significant obstacles to be overcome before the mail order retailer's window could be filled with lines already on the High Street, [as manufacturers of branded goods thought they would be lowering their tone to supply mail order companies, and retail shops did not want an invasion into their preserve].
> (2005: 62)

From the 1950s onwards, the mail-order companies entered into a ten-year battle with the high street as they attempted to attract the more affluent post-war consumer however, Coopey (2005) argues that the phenomenal growth of mail-order sales in the 1950s encouraged manufacturers of branded goods to rethink their positions, and they eventually agreed to be included. Burberry's acquisition by GUS was a brilliant strategic move, as it neatly sidestepped the need for negotiations and they simply added the company to their existing mail-order portfolio. Two other significant elements improved the profile and public reception to catalogue shopping: the shift from cash to credit (which arrived in Britain in the 1950s) and the transition from the club organizer to the agent. The agent was able to offer credit to customers, who in turn were able to receive goods even before the first instalment had been paid. This was seen as an important step in an era characterized by a generally cautious attitude towards the notion of independent credit for women, as Coopey and others observe

> Working class women, comprising the bulk of mail order's customers in this period could access 38 weeks credit via a simple transaction with a neighbour rather than exposing themselves to the risk of negative discrimination when applying for credit at a High Street store. (2005: 65)

As Coopey points out, the provision of a locally assessed credit system helped working class women to circumvent the traditional channels open to them – the High Street stores and department stores, and by avoiding these spaces they no longer felt what Skeggs (2008) describes as matter out of place. Skeggs argues that the store represents a space where working-class women feared they would be humiliated, or had already been humiliated, as they felt they lacked the requisite cultural capital, and asking for credit turned it into a site to be feared and avoided. The agency system also gave working-class women a safe haven from the tallymen, who offered quick cash on the doorstep but charged exorbitant rates of interest, but its two most important contributions were time-saving efficiencies, particularly as more women worked full-time, and an extended use of women's social networks at a local level, as the system provided a way in which they could exercise financial planning and a sense of prudency. Miller (1998) argues that thrift is a key value that underpins the way working-class women understand their shopping practices, and this characteristic was exploited to its maximum potential by Kay's and other catalogue providers, as it allowed customers to plan and budget for special, non-essential items including fashionable clothing. In common with other big mail-order companies, Kay's relied on its network of agents to assess potential clients' ability to pay, and the agents were usually the most trusted woman in the area. They were custodians of the catalogue, who drummed up trade with neighbours, friends and family, and had the ability to identify and assess extenuating circumstances for any of her clients including sudden job loss, or a death in the family. This assessment could only be done by someone with specific local knowledge who knew exactly who could and could not afford the weekly repayments, and was for all its apparent simplicity, a highly sophisticated financial system. This form of buying and selling continued until the 1980s, and situated the home shopping catalogue in a local context until other forms of credit – credit cards and store cards – were brought to the market. As applications for this type of credit were assessed through Credit Reference Agencies, this made the transactions anonymous and national, and in many ways this remoteness signalled the end of the agency systems' localism. Thrift (2005) argues that the use of coding – exemplified in credit profiling – limits our chances of negotiation, as the remote service has removed the possibility of making an account of ourselves, as it is automated and impersonal. The catalogue agents, with their expansive and intimate local knowledge, were phased out, and the heyday of catalogue shopping was effectively over, as by the end of the 1980s 'credit is freely available, most women have at least part-time jobs and it is far less common to live in a community close-knit enough for catalogues to be passed among neighbours' (Coopey et al., 2005: 70).

Home shopping declined in the 1990s, though this was initially masked by an increase in the number of agents; however they bought goods solely for their immediate family. In 1997, the Monopolies and Mergers Commission reported that although GUS were market leaders with 40.6 per cent of the UK mail-order market share, with Littlewoods following in second place with 27.9 per cent, all was not well

> However, by the end of the 90s, it was becoming clear, at least to City analysts, that GUS and Littlewoods, Britain's two largest mail order houses, were experiencing difficulties in adjusting to changing conditions. Though GUS had diversified in the mid-1990s, acquiring Argos, the high street catalogue retailer, and Experian, an information services provider, the performance of its mail order division was problematic. A dramatic fall of 70% in profits in 1999 prompted the observation that the time was fast approaching when GUS should perhaps bite the bullet, and close down. (Coopey et al., 2005: 69)

We know from Chapter 2 that Burberry had experienced financial difficulties in the mid-1990s, prompting Bravo's appointment to take control of the ailing company in 1997, but now its parent company was in jeopardy, and after nearly one hundred years of unparalleled success in the mail-order business, GUS had lost its way. Clearly GUS's other businesses were succeeding where their mail-order business failed to prosper, as in 2002 *Marketing Magazine* reported a £20 million investment at GUS to review and reinvigorate its marketing strategy, previously handled exclusively by McCann-Erickson Manchester. *Marketing Magazine* revealed that the GUS home shopping catalogue division was considering a 'youth overhaul', with catalogue launches aimed at a younger demographic, and that 'luxury goods brand Burberry' (Kleinman, 2002) was part of the deal. However, this initiative failed to give the corporation an edge over its competitors and as the online and e-commerce market geared up for growth, GUS sold its traditional home shopping division to the Barclay brothers in 2004.

After Burberry was successfully floated on the London Stock Exchange in 2002, they remained bound to the GUS conglomerate until a demerger formally separated them in 2005, but from the early years of the twenty-first century, they too had an eye on the youth market, and the *Daily Telegraph* reported that Bravo was keen to broaden its appeal.

> 'I would like to see more people able to buy into the brand', she says. She hints that the group is working on a range of clothing and accessories which will retail at slightly lower, more affordable prices. 'Burberry has the ability to broaden its audience. It will not be mass market or high street, but it could be more than a rarefied breed', she says. (Mills, 2000)

The success of the 2000 campaign featuring Moss meant that Burberry were in no doubt about the new direction they were taking ' "Getting our bikini on Kate Moss cut the average age of our customers by 30 years in one fell swoop," smiles Ms Bravo' (*Economist*, 2001). Though Burberry successfully attracted a younger demographic using the image of Moss in a bikini, what Bravo and brand consultants Baron & Baron may not have considered was the rigid hierarchy of the British class system, and when the same image also enticed a cross section of working-class consumers to the brand, they were viewed by the British media as being radically different to the Kay's catalogue customers. However, one particular demographic began to emerge in the UK media and a vivid image of the football hooligan and their attraction to Burberry became visible over the following four years, attracting headlines including 'Pubs Slap Ban on Burberry Lager Louts' (Sky News, 2004). But where did the link between Burberry and out-of-control behaviour emerge, and what made them choose Burberry? One potential source, dating back to the nineteenth century, came from the Scuttlers – teenage gangs who roamed Victorian Manchester, and who came from the poorest and most overcrowded districts in the newly industrialized city. They were not conventional criminals, but took pride in how aggressive they were, pride in their territory, and pride in their appearance and shared identity. Their distinctive neckerchief draws aesthetic parallels to the Burberry Nova check, and perhaps this formed a visual link to the company that was carried forward into the next century?

Andrew Davies's (2009) research into the Scuttlers, revealed that despite solely conducting their turf wars with other teenage gangs, they were widely feared by residents, business owners, religious and civic leaders. The fights were heavily reported in a plethora of newspapers in the north east of England, and a moral panic ensued throughout the 1870s and right up to the 1890s, as ever more harsh prison sentences were handed down to boys as young as twelve and thirteen, some of whom received fifteen to twenty-year jail terms.

The public outcry over the nineteenth-century Scuttlers was followed in the twentieth century by a new figure – the Mod, who emerged within British post-war youth culture. Here, newly affluent working-class teenagers spent their disposable income on luxury clothing, which they used as a way of what Hebdige describes as creating a 'parody of consumer society in which they were situated' (1975: 93). A promotional image for British R&B band Shotgun Express in 1966, shows Rod Stewart wearing a classic trench coat at the height of the Mod era. Stewart came from a working-class background and self-identified as a Mod, however the image tells us that the standard parka and mohair suit 'uniform' wasn't worn by everyone within the subculture, and young

Figure 4.2 Convicted Scuttler William Brooks (1870).
Image provided by Greater Manchester Police Museum and Archive.

working-class men often wore tailored clothing from long-established British clothing companies. Two years prior to the Shotgun Express image, Stewart was photographed wearing a Daks suit jacket (established in 1894) at one of his first live appearances at the London-based Marquee club. Stewart was only nineteen years old, but he states that his intention at that age was to dress 'like an English country gent' ('Imagine', BBC television, 2013). Stewart's background as a working-class teenager was typical of many – he was a reluctant pupil who left school at fifteen, and drifted through a range of dead-end jobs until he started to get paid regularly as a backing singer. Through he lacked educational capital he made up for this by constructing an image of himself that enhanced his cultural and symbolic capital through the character of an English Country Gent. Hebdige (1975) describes this style as 'expropriating', meanings given to objects borrowed from the dominant culture, and transforming them by the way they were worked into a new ensemble. So, Stewart's classic trench coat and Daks jacket were transformed into what Hebdige argues are oblique criticisms of the passive consumerism around them, as the Mods

> learned by experience (at school and work) to avoid direct confrontations where age, experience, economic and civil power would have told against them. The Mod dealt his blows by inverting and distorting images (of neatness, of short hair) so cherished by his employers and parents, to create a style, which while being overtly close to the straight world was nonetheless incomprehensible to it. (1975: 93)

Similarly, in the early 1970s, and taking cues from Mod culture came the suede heads, or what the *Sunday Times* dubbed the 'Crombie Boys'. Though the suede heads followed in the aftermath of the skinhead movement, they were very different in temperament as they eschewed violence, but they too wanted to look like 'gentlemen'. The suede heads adopted a more tailored aesthetic, and selected British company Crombie (established in 1805) as their label of choice. Crombie were a traditional men's outfitters, and the company were more closely associated with city businessmen than to suburban suede heads. Though many working-class consumers aspired to own a genuine Crombie, in hard financial times they could not afford the genuine products, and had to opt for imitations, as a double-page *Sunday Times* article from 1971 detailed.

> Meet the Crombie Boys
>
> The kids call these overcoats Crombies, but they are rarely the genuine article made from the celebrated Crombie cloth. Still, there is a touch of real class

tucked in the top pocket – a pure silk handkerchief. This gentlemanly fad started in London, swaggering out from the east end on to the football terraces where it was caught like measles and spread to places as far apart as Highgate and Barnes. Now you can see Crombie boys getting off the football specials from the midlands and the north. It's a look for boys (and a few girls) between 12 and 20 who want to give themselves a group identity that swings away from the aggressive look of skinheads and rockers; some south London Crombie boys have even been seen with rolled umbrellas. (*Sunday Times Magazine*, 1971)

The text in the article points out the importance of the right accessories – the silk handkerchief and the rolled umbrella – items borrowed from dominant culture that echo findings made by social scientist Frederic le Play (Crane, 2000) in nineteenth-century France, where he documents how working-class men – largely in urban settings – adopted the silk or satin tie, waistcoat and vest, styles firmly connected to the middle classes and the bourgeoisie. In 1970s Britain, many of those 'bourgeois' accessories were bought using mail-order catalogues, especially for working-class consumers on a tight budget, as well as those who lacked access to fashionable stores. On the Mod-to-Suedehead.net forum, Man-of-Mystery remarks

[This] reminds me a lot of some pictures I once saw in a mail-order catalogue (Littlewoods?) my mum had in about 1970. Obviously the mail order company was trying to cash in on trends observed on the street, but got there late. (mod-to-suedehead.net, 10 October 2013)

Some trends observed on the street included a new type of well-dressed gang, and one hundred years after the Scuttlers, came Birmingham City Football Club's Zulu Warriors, who were seen wearing designer clothing. The Zulu Warriors were highlighted in a programme broadcast by the British-based Bravo channel, who specialized in reality television programmes aimed at men aged twenty to forty. The station's image emanated partially from its tag line, 'Home of the Brave', and from its output, where a typical show was the Danny Dyer-fronted *The Real Football Factories* which was originally shown between May and June 2006. The programme responded to a new source of moral panic surrounding football hooligans in the early- to mid-2000s, and attempted to give an in-depth profile and history of football hooliganism and football firms using Dyer's on-screen persona as what Deans and Plunkett (2014) described as a working-class hard man to market the series. However, the stories of hooliganism and extreme behaviour masked a narrative of shared community, identity and camaraderie. The Real Football Factories examined the Zulu Warriors' role as an anti-racist gang comprising Black, Asian and white supporters in the early 1980s, who battled right-wing and British National Party fans at other clubs. The cultural diversity of this gang was matched by the uniformity of their clothing, which shows them wearing Burberry and Aquascutum clothes and accessories in several personal photographs. In one image from 1982, three young Black men are seen wearing a Burberry flat cap, a Burberry trilby and a Burberry scarf, and another image shows a group of friends on a train on match day also wearing the distinctive Burberry Nova check. In Dyer's documentary, one of the original Zulu Warriors, David George, is interviewed and he explained their choice 'We went with all our colours, our favourite clothes and our favourite music' (The Real Football Factories, 2006). For George, the group identity made it clear to other members of the firm – which at its height during the 1980s was over four hundred – that 'these were my brothers', and the instantaneous recognition, mirroring the nineteenth-century Scuttlers, gave each member a feeling of solidarity. Criminologist James Treadwell suggests other key reasons for appropriating labels like Burberry as brands of choice in the early 1980s

> For football hooligans the underpinning logic of adopting expensive clothes was avoidance of police attention – and designer ware and comparatively more expensive modes of transport ['intercity' rather than football special trains] ensured this. Moreover, they could readily identify others dressed like them. (2008: 124)

However, within the public domain, the sight of four hundred young men engaged in battle – however noble the cause, was terrifying. Burberry's polarized image emerged from this context in the UK and has effectively remained in an altered state – away from the luxury and premium fashion sector, at a local level since then.

The national face of Burberry's downward trajectory began in November 2003 when a bar in Aberdeen refused entry to a woman with a Burberry handbag and umbrella as part of their 'no Burberry' dress code stipulations. Some publicans continued to make a connection between the brand and incidents of football hooliganism, however in this case it was the *misrecognition* of the woman as a football casual that attracted headlines in *The Scottish Herald* (Chiesa and Porch, 2003) the *Publican* (2003) the *Daily Mail* (Madeley, 2003) *The Guardian* (Finch 2003) *British Vogue* (2003) and marketing and media title, *The Drum* (2003). The Guardian reported that many bar owners in Scotland felt that 'Burberry has become the badge of thuggery' (Finch, 2003). Press coverage on the Burberry ban in Aberdeen eventually trailed off, however another ban issued in the summer of 2004 by two Leicester-based bars, the Varsity and the Parody, who refused entry to anyone wearing Burberry, reignited media interest. The Varsity and the Parody were part of the Barracuda Group who ran a network of 154 venues throughout the UK, and news of their ban also went from being a local news story to one of national significance, and was covered in newspapers including *The Guardian* (Oliver, 2004), *The Telegraph* (Hall, 2004), *PR Week* (Robertson, 2004) and featured on Sky News and the BBC. All media outlets reiterated the original press report from the Leicester Mercury that the ban on drinkers wearing Burberry was an attempt to 'crack down on violence' (BBC News, 2004b). The Barracuda Group's initiative was duplicated by bars, pubs and clubs up and down the UK and highly visible notices appeared outside city centre licensed premises, predominantly those attracting a younger demographic, barring entry to anyone wearing Burberry. Informally, the police got involved in identifying potential troublemakers, and the link between Burberry and hooliganism persisted, as these posts on the Police Specials Forum confirm. 'Pinky', responding to the article in the Leicester Mercury, writes

> I do Hudds Town Football matches regularly – more or less every home game – and you know who the troublemakers are by the labels they wear – and they are LABELS, in the 'Look at Me!!!' way of wearing them.
>
> You can spot the 'hooligans' as they wear the Fred Perry polo shirts and jeans, with Burberry caps, and you can see the younger element, the 'wannabes', wearing labels on everything. I saw one lad (approx 17) at the Town v Hartlepool match the other week with Burberry baseball cap, t-shirt with BURBERRY on it in big letters. (Police Specials Forum, 2004)

Two days later 'Zulu', another officer, responded

> The sad thing is that the majority of 'burberry' items worn in the High Street are not even genuine Burberry, just imitation. I was talking to a lad in custody (in for burglary) who asked me if our Stabvests come in Burberry. (Police Specials Forum, 2004)

The posts from the Special Constables mark an important distinction as although they are informal messages from colleague to colleague, both officers represent an official element of dominant culture and their messages are visible in the public domain. After the deluge of comment and criticism, Burberry issued a statement dismissing the story from the Leicester Mercury, stating that it was 'a localised issue and to be honest it's actually quite insignificant in the face of the brand's global appeal' (BBC News, 2004). However, by October 2004 Burberry were no longer in a position to deny the fracture occurring within the brand, and when their Finance Director Stacey Cartright was interviewed in the financial section of *The Independent*, she admitted that

> 'We're missing the UK domestic consumer ... the UK market has been sluggish, particularly in central London.' She admitted that the adverse publicity over the popularity of the group's trademark check with 'chavs' – an emerging class of twentysomething urbanites who favour designer labels but lack the social status of traditional luxury goods customers – was probably behind the fall in demand. 'It won't have helped, I'm sure', Ms Cartwright added. (Mesure, 2004)

The sensational headlines and public dress code bans effectively polarized Burberry's image in the UK. The company attempted to reassure investors and consumers by implementing remedial action to reposition the brand away from its trademark check after the 'beige-and-black motif was hijacked by the likes of football hooligans' (Mesure, 2004). A BBC television show, *The Money Programme* confirmed this and reported that Burberry 'had removed the checked baseball caps from sale and reduced the visibility of their distinctive pattern. Three years ago it was on a fifth of all products. By 2004 it was on less than 5%' (Bothwell, 2005). But were these changes already too late? Had the Burberry brand already leaked nationwide and become part of a different ideology, where its brand associations now included the football hooligan. It was hardly surprising then, that an image from 2006 shown on Bravo television of a young man wearing a Burberry Nova check jacket being arrested by two police officers was, for some viewers, business as usual as it captured all that was 'wrong' about luxury brands being appropriated by the 'wrong' consumers. For Burberry, it highlighted the radical difference between its local image and global profile, and in the UK, it made a clear connection in the public domain between working-class consumption of Burberry and criminal behaviour. A cycle of appropriation started by the nineteenth-century Scuttlers, the mid-1960s Mod, the 1970s suede head and the Burberry-wearing Zulu Warriors in the early 1980s made it clear at a local level at least, that this way of dressing not only helped to identify rivals, but it also boosted cultural capital through ownership of high prestige items admired by peers. Burberry was not the first brand to be used as a way of what Moor describes as 'buying cultural capital in objectified form through brand name commodities' (2007: 134) but it was likely to be the most expensive, and so when an emerging 'chav' culture started to be connected to the brand, the media questioned how they could afford luxury fashion on an income that consisted primarily of welfare benefits. But were they even attempting to buy cultural capital?

'Chav Scum'

'Chavs' argues Jones (2011) are unremittingly portrayed as thick, violent and criminal, and differ from what was perceived as an older, more respectable working class. 'Chav' culture was effectively formed by a rising inequality that led to an increasingly segregated society in Britain, where a 'traditional' male-dominated heavy industry infrastructure had been slowly diminishing. Starved of conventional work, and with little hope of secure employment, many turned to the welfare system, and were subsequently viewed as what Lawler (2005) describes as a workshy underclass facing a lifetime on benefits. Jones (2011) also argues that the Conservative government's demeaning attitude towards trade unions helped to strip the working classes of their public voice so that the middle class effectively became the new decision-making class. However, 'chav' culture wasn't solely a product of Tory legislation, as New Labour compounded the problem as far back as 1997, stating 'we're all middle-class now', which heralded an era of neo-liberalism.

Against this background of political, economic and social change, perceptions of Burberry altered to take account of a new influx of 'urban chav' consumers, and Burberry, or more accurately the Nova check, became the aesthetic focal point of 'chav' culture. Consumers and the media reacted swiftly to the connection between the luxury brand and a demographic they felt had no business wearing Burberry, however what is distinctive is the *level* of protest: the football hooliganism from an earlier era was mutely accepted as they occupied a very particular domain – the football terraces and streets surrounding the ground – however 'chav' culture was ubiquitous, appearing frequently in the news and entertainment media. Jones (2011) argues that 'chav' as a pejorative term is potentially the last form of prejudice, but one in which all classes participate, and where racist or homophobic hate speech is a criminal offence, 'chav bashing' was socially and politically acceptable. *The Telegraph*'s financial reporter joined in the abuse with this headline

> Burberry brand tarnished by 'chavs'
>
> Burberry, the luxury goods group, has seen a sharp decline in UK sales due to the popularity of its trademark camel check among so-called 'chavs', a pejorative term for a low-income social group obsessed with brand names, cheap jewellery and football. Retailers who stock Burberry products say there is a growing negative association with the brand as the national obsession with chav culture has flourished. (Hall, 2004)

The financial report is clear about its intent to show how brand associations can impact sales and revenue, but Hall's article nonetheless demonstrates a negative appraisal, and he uses derogatory language throughout the article. Two posts on the consumer site reviewcentre.com go further in their criticism of 'chavs' adopting Burberry as their brand of choice: 'I urge the company to drop this design and disassociate itself from this class of society' (Andy123, Review Centre, 3 September 2004).

> The founders of Burberry must be so annoyed that their brand has become the staple diet of chavs across the country. They put in so much hard work coming up with designs only for them to be adopted by idiots and Neanderthals as a calling card. (Lcarlisle, Review Centre, 21 February 2008)

The two posts – written four years apart – show how entangled Burberry had become with a negative symbolic value of 'chav' culture, and they also demonstrate how British consumers became angry in relation to what they perceived as an undeserving marginal group essentially hijacking an important, symbolic-making and historic brand. But why did Andy123 and Lcarlise care so much about Burberry's reputation? Lawler (2005) suggests that it may well have been middle-class disgust, a powerful affect aroused when they sensed that what they considered good taste, in which they had invested, had been violated. Burberry could not follow Andy123's advice and 'drop' the Nova check design, as it was one of their biggest brand assets, however the company faced a dilemma: how could it defend itself from the onslaught of what Lawler (2005) describes as disgusting subjects without appearing to be judgmental, which in itself had the potential to damage brand value? The social, political and economic climate between 2004 and 2008 – when the posts were first published, was characterized by what Lawler describes as a narrative of decline, where

> a once respectable working-class which held progressive principles and knew its assigned purpose [had] now disappeared, to be either absorbed into an allegedly-expanding middle class, or consigned to a workless and workshy underclass which lacks taste, is politically retrogressive, dresses badly, and above all, is prey to a consumer culture. (2005: 433)

Burberry's silence may have been sufficient ammunition for UK consumers and the media to respond on their behalf, as 'chavs' had already been widely assigned a role as the repellent *other*, and no one was likely to come to their defence. Andy123's level of disgust prompts him to post another comment the same day, showing how his repugnance manifested itself in his description of the 'chav' aesthetic and lifestyle

> It continually keeps a smile on my face seeing the burgeoning peasant
>
> underclass trying to look stylish by wearing it! To be fair, when this design came out it was probably seen as very classy and upmarket for high flyers who wanted to be seen as being successful. Now, unfortunately, the masses have adopted it as a form of bling to go with their hideous gold clown pendants, Von Bitch copy t-shirts, trakkie bottoms, Rockport boots and fatherless new-borns sporting Claire accessory creole earrings! Please, I implore you! Drop this design and disassociate yourselves as far away from these kinds of lowlife chavscum. (Andy123, Review Centre, 2004)

Andy123's comments about 'high flyers' versus a 'burgeoning peasant underclass' (a phrase taken directly from 'The Little Book of Chavs' Bok, 2004) shows the polarity of Burberry's position in the UK where, metaphorically speaking, one class is in the ascendant – the 'high' flyer – while the underclass is facing downwards, but it also illustrates Lawler's argument about how personal aesthetics can be directly translated into a sense of morality, where 'chavs' are viewed as having no taste and where 'those positioned as lacking "taste" can also be positioned as morally lacking … This is precisely why working-class people are so readily judged by their appearance' (Lawler, 2005: 441).

Andy123's post simultaneously piles on the hate speech, but also references what Skeggs argues is 'coding a whole way of life that is deemed to be repellant' (2003: 2). In contrast, the 'old' working classes, though once viewed as a scourge, were now seen as noble and respectable, and it was 'chavs' who were viewed as scroungers. Again, the question for Burberry was how to extricate the brand from this situation without damaging its value, however the company were braced for more bad news, as their situation was further complicated by an increasingly widespread production and adoption of counterfeit Burberry clothing.

F for fake

It is likely that many low-income consumers could not afford authentic Burberry products, making the Special Constables' comments about imitations particularly apposite. The rise in counterfeit goods troubled Burberry, particularly in proximity to working-class consumption of the brand, many of whom sought alternatives to expensive, genuine products, and it was this consumer group's on-going search that proved to be a significant driver in the increasingly widespread production of fakes. Rose Marie Bravo had attempted to stem the flow of fake goods to the market in the late 1990s, however the company's complex licensing agreements with global manufacturers meant that her initiative was difficult for the brand to police effectively. It did however, alert the company to the importance of regulating their own intellectual property rights and protect their distinctiveness through a legal framework by attempting to exclude others from using the same designs. Lash and Urry (1994) argue that in post-Fordist work, where design is central, company value is primarily about acquisition, packaging and marketing intellectual property (IP) rights, in other words Burberry's distinctive trademarks – particularly the Nova check and the Equestrian Knight logo – put a financial value onto the company. However, it was those visible and easily recognizable elements that attracted working class consumers, and not the more obscure and upmarket Burberry Prorsum line, which had few familiar features. The check and the knight are the elements most used in fakes, so there was a significant danger of diminishing brand equity as the flood of fakes entered the UK market.

Trademarks were originally introduced to protect consumers from goods being 'passed off' as originals, however as IP law became more internationalized in the contemporary global market, May and Sell (2005) argue that the laws are increasingly used to protect revenue streams and money spent on marketing, and have significantly less consumer focus. Fake Burberry products are offered for sale on eBay and in street markets up and down the UK, and a study carried out by lawyers Davenport Lyons and Ledbury Research in 2007 showed that Burberry lay in third place, after Louis Vuitton and Gucci, as the most copied brand in the UK (Cable, 2007). Jonathan Cable at *Reuters* (2007) reported that the IPR division at Burberry 'devoted a lot of resources to eBay and worked closely with the site, ending more than 30,000 auctions last year', and according to the UK's Anti-Counterfeiting Group, shoppers hoping to buy a designer bargain on eBay or from a discount website are taken in by convincing sites and prices that reflect a premium brand, however as IP laws no longer extend their protection to customers, Laura Chesters writing in *The Independent* (2012) pointed out that goods suspected of being fakes are intercepted at airport hubs and dockyards and destroyed on site, after which the firm sends a letter to the buyer telling them they have bought a fake from an illegal seller, and the customer is left empty handed.

Conversely, Mishcon de Reya, lawyers representing some of the luxury brands against the counterfeiters, report that monitoring sales of fake products has become increasingly difficult, as the business has expanded rapidly from a small number of retailers on the high street, to a multiplicity of sellers trading from home. Chesters (2012) reported that while the source of counterfeit products is widespread, the Far East is 'at the core of the problem', but discovers that 'it is more common for China to be the manufacturer rather than the consumer of copies', and it seems that although China's high-profile markets are attractive to bargain hunters, they are primarily aimed at the international tourist trade, and middle-class Chinese consumers shun all but the originals.

One of the biggest issues for luxury brands are the global distribution chains, and according to Jeremy Herzog, head of the intellectual property group at Mishcon de Reya, fakes can even find their way to legitimate distribution channels. More disturbing though, is the lack of control, as brands cannot regulate the pricing or the invaluable consumer experience outside authorized retailers. The brand-protection company MarkMonitor argues that fakes have direct cost implications for consumers, as firms have to raise their prices in order to differentiate their products from the fakes. Despite the work attempting to differentiate the genuine from the imitation, fakes can easily be mistaken for a legitimate product, and this anonymous post at reviewcentre. com shows how the writers' sense of pride in owning an original Burberry shirt turns to dismay at the easy availability of fakes for sale in his own neighbourhood, lessening the impact of his authentic product, and potentially diminishing his local status.

Written on: 07/08/2006 by Anonymous101

Good Points

My Burberry casual shirt is the favourite item in my wardrobe. My girlfriend bought me it about three years ago and although it is a little threadbare now, it still manages to turn a few heads when I go on a night out. A lot of my friends can't afford Burberry so I feel far superior to them.

Bad Points

Burberry is now very famous and is widely available throughout the UK. Even Doggy market has been selling the brand recently. I do however, worry that all these baseball style caps, t-shirts and jackets being sold near my house will deter from the impact my shirt once made. (Review Centre, 7 August 2006)

The author of this post is clearly worried about the impact of fakes on his elite reputation in the neighbourhood, as he is proud to wear a genuine Burberry shirt, and it's a point argued by Treadwell who points out that 'the ability to acquire core items most admired by peers' (2008: 124) remains a key element in building and maintaining local status. It's not just fans of Burberry who are worried about the association fakes bring to the brand – the significance of the cheap imitation has permeated British culture more widely, as this post from 'Silly Sausage' on SecularCafé.org illustrates

> The problem with Burberry is, as Pendaric says, all the knock off gear. I don't know if Burberry makes those awful shell suits or they're knock-offs – I don't think chavs will be in a hurry to ditch the Burberry (or knock-off) gear though, and that's part of the problem. While they continue to wear it, and people know they are wearing it, it will never have the same appeal in this country. (secularcafe.org, 26 January 2011b)

This post underlines how difficult it is to differentiate between fakes and genuine Burberry products, as the Nova check pattern has become part of another, fetishistic style at a local level. Burberry doesn't manufacture shell suits, but the counterfeiters have seen a gap in the market and produced clothing featuring the Nova check in order to satisfy consumer demand, however those same consumers have then adapted the clothing to fit their lifestyles, for example, by wearing a baggy hooded top with a pair of tracksuit bottoms so it resembles an entire suit. This sense of reworking is evident in Hebdige's study of Mod culture where he examines

> the way objects and things were borrowed by the Mods from the world of consumer commodities, and their meaning transformed by the way they were worked into a new ensemble. This involved expropriating the meanings given to things by the dominant consumer culture, and incorporating them in ways which expressed sub-cultural rather than dominant values. (1975: 87)

This way of dressing, then, was no longer a way of buying status within dominant culture, but a way of expressing sub-cultural values, and this was and continues to be a paradox for Burberry, as the 'chav' consumer group have moved away from what Hayward and Yar (2006) describe as the charade of self-improvement, and are instead preoccupied by what Treadwell describes as the 'excessive consumption of some fashion brand items' (2008: 121). In a long history of cultural appropriation, working-class culture has effectively shaped a new pathway, where borrowing from the dominant culture means reassigning values attached to luxury brands, and no longer signals a desire to be 'better'.

The bad object

Where working-class men's consumption of Burberry was tied to an image of football hooliganism and misconduct, the now infamous image of Danniella Westbrook and her child clad head-to-toe in Burberry became emblematic of all that was perceived as 'bad' about working-class women's consumption of the brand, as it was, and still is, widely considered to be tasteless. Westbrook's own image became indelibly linked to failure – failed relationships, failed cosmetic surgeries and multiple failed drug rehabilitations – and she has become a figure of what Tyler and Bennett (2010) describe as 'celebrity chav'. The image dates from 2002, however UK news media continue to hold her personally responsible for the potential downfall of Burberry and banner headlines including 'When it comes to Burberry, Danniella Westbrook has a lot to answer for' (Carpenter, 2011) are not uncommon. Certainly, Westbrook's personhood as a key 'celebrity chav' communicates what Tyler and Bennett describe as 'the excessive embodiment of class hatred' (2010: 379). Why was Westbrook singled out and pilloried so heavily for wearing Burberry? Prior to this image she was known in the media as the celebrity with a cocaine habit so severe that she required surgery for a collapsed septum. After this photograph appeared, she became what Tyler and Bennett describe as the 'bad object', and a single focus for public rage. They also point out that 'many of the social networking sites, blogs and discussion groups devoted to the analysis of celebrity behavior express intense, hyperbolic hatred and aversion rather than love or admiration. Hatred can be a community-forming attachment to a "bad" object' (2010: 377). Westbrook fulfilled the bad object role completely and she continues to follow a well-trodden path of other 'celebrity chavs' including self-penned exposés of a rise to stardom, and regular appearances on confessional and 'reality' television programmes. However, the principal and most public sign of a 'celebrity chav' is breast augmentation surgery that Tyler and Bennett argue is a 'key signifier of working class female celebrity associated with glamour modeling and pornography, especially when surgically enhanced' (2010: 385–6). Indeed the 'celebrity chav' lifestyle is built around this form of excess – too much silicone, too much misery, too much fat, too much money and too much poverty. It was this sense of overabundance that made Westbrook a clear target for the media and online communities, who did not denigrate her for wearing Burberry, but for wearing this *quantity* of the distinguishing pattern, which has been repeatedly described as tasteless.

Lawler points out that this sense of tastelessness has a long history within the working classes, arguing that

> Everything is saturated with meaning: their clothes, their bodies, their houses, all are assumed to be markers of some 'deeper', pathological form of identity. This identity is taken to be ignorant, brutal and tasteless. As in eugenically-inspired (often retouched) photographs popular at the turn of the Twentieth Century, white working-class people's actions and appearance are made to *mean*: they are made to indicate signs of ignorance, stupidity, tastelessness. An assumed ignorance and immorality is read off from an aesthetic which is constituted as faulty. (2005: 436)

The media focused on Westbrooks' aesthetic and found it overwhelmingly faulty, and her outfit choice for a single day effectively cast her as ignorant, stupid and tasteless forever. UK newspapers including *The Guardian*, the *Daily Mail*, *The Express* and *The Economist* did not hold back with their brutal appraisals of Westbrook's appearance, as this piece from *The Guardian* illustrates

> But, there is one image in the history of Burberry that sticks in the mind, with the same lingering cloy as a half-sucked toffee: a picture of the actress Danniella Westbrook clad top to toe in Burberry check: the hat, the skirt, the scarf, her baby dressed up to match, as if she had gorged herself upon it, rolled about in it like a pig in muck. It looked like the end of the much-heralded Burberry revival: the Burberry check had become the ultimate symbol of nouveau rich naff. (Barton and Pratley, 2004)

The Guardian uses an enflamed language that seems at odds with a liberal newspaper, showing how pervasive and unchallenged hate speech towards the white working classes had become. Westbrook's proximity to the brand created a sullying effect on Burberry, and caused writers to hold her responsible for making it a 'symbol of the nouveau rich naff'. Four years later, Liz Jones, writing in the *Daily Mail* showed how the media still dwelt on Westbrook: 'The day that former soap star Danniella Westbrook and her daughter stepped out head to toe in Burberry sounded the death knell for the company's credibility' (Jones, 2008).

Though it's less surprising to see more extreme language in the right-wing *Daily Mail*, nonetheless tying Westbrook to the death knell of a company is excessive, however it was an article in the *The Express* (2011) that took Westbrook to task not only for her choice of clothes, but for her life choices, effectively returning the text to a description of the poor at the turn of the twentieth century.

> Many will remember the occasion in 2004 when the ex-soap actress – then best known for her nose-eroding cocaine addiction – was photographed on the streets with her daughter dressed head-to-toe in the label. We're talking everything from matching skirts and bag down to baby buggy covers. At the time it had become almost a byword for 'chav' and Danniella's overdosing of the trademark check exemplified all that had gone wrong with the British brand. Anyone deciding to don its outfits feared for their sartorial credibility. (Carpenter, 2011)

The corrosive tone of the article effectively turns Westbrook into a caricature of deformity and unthinking excess, but the overall text invites us to tacitly agree with the writer and become a fellow arbiter of what constitutes good taste, which Lawler contends is a long-running argument and that 'the many expressions of disgust at white working-class existence within the British media and other public forums [cut] across conventional Left/Right distinctions – have largely passed without comment' (2005: 429). Lawler (2005) also examines what constitutes a 'common understanding', which in this case was Westbrook's degree of tastelessness, as there seems to be no public sense that she is *not* tasteless, and consequently we are invited to join in with the criticism, and to accept it without question. Westbrook continues to be criticized from multiple sources – the fashion press, news media, celebrity gossip and entertainment magazines, online communities, the financial press – and using Lawler's (2005) examination of what is respectably say-able within a cultural space, we find that even the finance pages use Westbrook as the 'bad object', as this article from *The Economist* shows

> By the early 2000s the company's distinctive camel-coloured check had become the uniform of the 'chav', the stereotypical white working-class delinquent looking for trouble. [When Daniella Westbrook, a soap actress, was photographed with the Burberry check adorning herself, her daughter and her pushchair, the brand's elite reputation seemed to be lost.] (*Economist Online*, 2011)

Though it's important for financial analysts to pinpoint any underlying social causes for economic upheaval, *The Economist* uses language that belittles its target – the white working classes become 'delinquents' and Westbrook is not an actor, but a more diminutive 'soap actress' (or as the *Daily Mail* puts it 'former soap star', while *The Express* opt for 'ex-soap actress'), but who is nonetheless capable of single-handedly depriving Burberry of its elite reputation. And though it is impossible to buy cultural capital, the same commentators also point out that even with financial resources at her disposal, Westbrook still fails to achieve a level of respectability, a point Lawler takes issue with, arguing that since respectability is

> coded as an inherent feature of 'proper' femininity, working-class women must constantly guard against being dis-respectable, but no matter how carefully they do this, they are always at risk of being judged as wanting by middle-class observers. And this is a double jeopardy since if working-class women can be rendered disgusting by dis-respectability and excess, they have also been rendered comic or disgusting in their attempts to be respectable. (Lawler, 2005: 387)

Equally, Westbrook failed at what Skeggs describes as 'passing' – using make up and dressing-up skills in order to 'display the desire not to pass as working class' (1997: 84). Those same skills – when they didn't work – were used to vilify Westbrook, as the context then becomes an issue of social mobility. The underlying critique becomes an assumption that Westbrook used Burberry clothing to 'escape' her working-class life, however Tyler and Bennett remind us that this is also likely to end in failure, as dominant culture weighs in with a cautionary narrative that accompanies the 'celebrity chav', and assumes that the outcome of transgressing class boundaries will be both 'difficult and undesirable' (2010: 389). In every way, Westbrook became the object on which to attach class rage, frustration and hate, however, what Burberry must have struggled with is that while any number of anonymous men behaving badly whilst wearing the Nova check could be dismissed, Westbrook was higher profile and could not be ignored so easily. The media storm surrounding her overtook the outrage and moral panic generated by the brand's link to football hooliganism, and though Westbrook had not committed a crime, the consequences of her decision to dress herself and her infant in Burberry, were in many ways worse as they burrowed into the very core of the company's values that in many of their Annual Reports claimed to embrace a meritocratic ethos. It is clear from Westbrook's experience that a resolutely inflexible class distinction was in place around Burberry, and though she had worked her way from obscurity to become a well-known actor, her lack of cultural capital held her back. Burberry, even when put on the spot, defended the company's wide appeal, as this interview with Creative Director Christopher Bailey in the *Daily Mail* demonstrates: 'And while Bailey, talking about his label's chavdom, is keen not to sound elitist – "I'm proud we had such a democratic appeal", he has been instrumental in returning to the brand its coolness' (Jones, 2008).

Though it's clear that Westbrook would not have a role in returning Burberry to its coolness, her attempt to dress in a brand she perceived as high value in order to stand out seems logical, and as Berlant argues 'an aesthetically expressed desire to be *somebody* in a world where the default is being nobody or, worse, being presumptively *all wrong*' (2000: 3) speaks for the harsh treatment meted out by the press and online communities who presumed her to be 'all wrong', as this post from Matty on SecularCafé.org illustrates 'ah daniella mononostril westbrook. interesting case, a straight up chavvete who "done well enough" to buy the real shit' (secularcafe.org, 23 January 2011a). Westbrook was indeed an interesting case, as she co-existed as a publicly owned celebrity – albeit a 'celebrity chav', and as an authentic working-class woman, and this seemed to multiply the quantity of criticism aimed at her. The subtext in Matty's comment carries an assumption that as Westbrook earned higher than average wages, she could afford to buy authentic Burberry clothes, so there was no excuse not the buy 'the real shit'. Similar responses awaited other working-class women who wore Burberry, like this comment from Kelly Owls on Football Forums in response to the Leicestershire-based 'Pub-goers face Burberry ban' story on the 20 August 2004

> Kelly Owls (23 August 2004)
> I got a burberry scarf -> £35
> I got a pink Von Dutch cap -> £45
> I got a blue Von Dutch cap -> £60
> I got some gold Nike Shox -> £110
>
> Does this make me a bad person?'
>
> Jagielka (23 August 2004)
> 'No, it just makes you a tasteless one. (FootballForums.net, 2004)

Kelly Owl's rhetorical question is well argued and assumes a preferred answer, however Jagielka's response ducks the obvious retort – that owning particular fashion brands could make anyone a 'bad' person – but instead uses a default reaction of tastelessness, turning it into an archetypal, gendered response.

Partington argues that a sense of division can be traced back to a period after 1945.

> The working class has been perceived as divided in the period after the second World War, between those on 'the margins' (who are thought to reject commodities or 'subvert' their values) and the mainstream (thought to consume passively). For instance (masculinized) sub-cultural 'style' is distinguished from

(feminized) mass cultural 'fashion'. While working-class women's activities have been associated with devalued cultural practices, male working-class culture has enjoyed the status of 'subversion' on the grounds that the commodity is either refused, or creatively 'appropriated' – as in bricolage. (1992: 149)

Hebdige's (1975) argument, that the Mods' oblique criticisms were aimed at the 'passive consumerism' around them, and his description of 'creative appropriation' as a way of subverting meanings given by dominant culture, supports Partington's (1992) argument about how 'marginal style' is seen as superior and a form of dress primarily attributed to men. We see this male-female divide in this post from 'Legs from Leeds' – a dedicated female consumer eager to share her positive views and experience of Burberry at the online consumer site reviewcentre.com, however she finds herself the focus of criticism, and clashes with a male reviewer.

By legs from leeds on 1st Sep 2004

User Ratings

Goods purchased and cost	Overcoat £500, duffle £595, watch £250
Quality of service	10/10
Layout of shop	10/10
Value for money	10/10
Overall rating	10/10
Recommended	Yes

Good Points
Burberry is the best

Bad Points
Expensive not many stockists in leeds

General Comments
I love Burberry you can't beat it for style and class when I'm out with my mum and two grandsons and we are all wearing burberry that's a head turner some people snigger but that's usually the clampets that can't afford Burberry I have socks shoes 2 overcoats 2 dufflecoats trousers jeans T-shirts, blouses, belts, hats, scarfs, gloves, sunglasses, 5 bags, purse, 4 keyrings and a watch so I know what im talking about Burberry real class we travel far and wide for ours. (Review Centre, 1 September 2004)

Legs from Leeds is overwhelmingly loyal to the brand, and we can see she has committed significant financial resources to buying clothing and accessories from Burberry. There is a clear sense of pride as she makes an inventory of her purchases within a public domain, but she also shows a clear understanding that not everyone at a local level understands her choices. A few months after her initial post, a comment from another online reviewer appeared in response to Legs's appraisal.

Comment by oldfart on 31st Dec 2004

I have a very nice Burberry trenchcoat which I bought from Burberry's in Regent Street about 15 years ago to replace the one that got pinched while I was having dinner at the House of Commons. Just goes to show that you couldn't trust anyone even then. I'm very fond of that trenchcoat and it's still in excellent condition. I had no idea that Burberry had such a huge following these days. People used to buy their products because they were of very high quality, I think even HMQ used to wear a Burberry headscarf on occasion. It would appear that today people buy Burberry for reasons of fashion, which usually results in the quality of the product coming down. There are so many good quality clothes out there, why bother to drape the entire family from head to foot in Burberry. You are inviting opinions so, to be quite frank, I think it's a bit of a tacky thing to do. You might have a bit of money but you may not have any taste or style'. (Oldfart, December 2004)

'Oldfart' carefully constructs an image of himself as a Burberry connoisseur; he lets us know he has dinner at the House of Commons, indicating that he's comfortable in a traditional base of authority and has personal links within a seat of power; he references 'fashion', distinguishing it, as Partington (1992) argues, as a feminized element of mass culture, and positions it as a lower status pre-occupation. What he makes abundantly clear, however, is that in his judgement Legs from Leeds displays a sense of tastelessness, and that she has no business 'draping the entire family in Burberry'. Oldfart harks back to a consumer culture of the past, in which identity was defined by rank, status, occupation and gender, and he seems bewildered that Burberry has moved into contemporary consumer culture that places an emphasis on signifying the cultural qualities of goods that reflect the knowledge, tastes, habits and preferences of consumers within an advanced economy. However, where dominant culture usually triumphs, on this occasion Legs is prepared for him, and reasserts herself in a robust and adversarial exchange of opinions.

Comment by legs on 4th Jan 2005

We are a working class family who happen to love burberry. We are not rich but I don't drink, gamble or smoke. My vice is burberry. I dont want my grandsons to look like most other kids walking round in a pair of tracky bottoms and a football shirt. I have taste and my grandsons have style. We don't wear it as a fashion thing. As you stated in your review you bought a trench coat 15 years ago, I've just bought a black trenchcoat. Fashion lasts 6 months not 15 years. (Legs from Leeds, January 2005)

Legs clearly feels strongly about the brand – strong enough to compel her to write a review about it, and having posted it, prompted her to revisit the site and respond to visitor comments. She constructs herself as someone responsible with money – she doesn't 'drink, gamble or smoke' and rejects the female spendaholic stereotype, or someone who is gullible and easily seduced by adverts. What is implicit in almost all the reviews on the reviewcentre.com bulletin board is a sense of misplacement, particularly when working class consumers are thought to be consuming the 'wrong' things, or consuming them in the 'wrong' way. After his remarks about the House of Commons and 'HMQ', Oldfart is clearly trying to outrank Legs: he sees himself as the intellectual, the person able to make judgments on others, and though he's clearly annoyed at Legs's lack of cultural capital, he is unable to voice his frustration coherently. Skeggs articulates succinctly on his behalf on why he has become so enraged about Burberry being bought by the 'wrong' people.

> Attributing negative value to the working class is a mechanism for attributing value to the middle-class self (such as making oneself tasteful through judging others to be tasteless). So, it is not just a matter of using some aspects of the culture of the working class to enhance one's value, but also maintaining the position of judgment to attribute value, which assigns the other as immoral, repellent, abject, worthless, disgusting, even disposable. (2005: 977)

Within British class structure, Legs's lack of cultural capital would have assigned her as 'other' within a dominant and symbolic national level, however Skeggs (1997) argues that all forms of capital are context specific, and though Legs from Leeds is not part of an elite group in a national context, she is at a local level. Legs carefully documents the price of her Burberry goods in order to differentiate them from fakes; she is critical of the way 'most other kids' in her neighbourhood dress, and dismissive of those who are critical of her clothing choices; she is aware that she's created a look that attracts attention which in turn means she has set herself apart from others in her own habitus. However, despite the expensive purchases, she is unlikely to command much in the way of economic capital, and though she may not possess legitimate forms of cultural capital, she is aware of what is seen as legitimate taste. Bourdieu (1986) argues that taste, an acquired cultural competence, is used to legitimize social differences, and that taste functions to make those social distinctions, but Legs shows us how those distinctions are made moment-to-moment, and on a micro level. Legs's refusal to be positioned without power takes the form of her ongoing fight back in her own neighbourhood, and her assertiveness in the face of Oldfarts's belittling comments. However, Legs's fundamental problem is that she has invested in Burberry as a sign of taste, and has bought into a brand image created by the company. What may trouble her is the fact that the brand doesn't have a fixed meaning, and that what she thought clearly signified 'good taste' has been positioned in other ways.

Conclusions

Burberry's connection to the working classes can be dated back to the mid-nineteenth century when the company made smocks for local agricultural workers, and re-emerged within consumer culture through a mail-order catalogue in post-war Britain. We see how this helped the company to reach a large-scale consumer group who were viewed, and viewed themselves, as being respectable. However, after Rose Marie Bravo introduced lower-priced items into the collection – a bikini, a bandana and a baseball cap, we saw how this status changed, as each of these items embodied distinct characteristics that were polar opposites of the sturdy outerwear the company were famous for. However, they were very attractive not only to a younger demographic, but to working-class consumers. The change to the product line caused Burberry to present particularly uneven, and sometimes contradictory brand values, as in the early days of the company's rebranding, and especially between 2000–04, Burberry's outward-facing communication strategy showcased a series of narratives around the new products that were inconsistent with a brand essence encompassing 'quintessentially British outerwear' (Burberry Annual Report, 2007-08) with images including the errant hen party guest, the shoplifter's accomplice, and out-of-control night-clubbing women. Did Moss's working-class identity combined with staged reality images and the new product line attract not only Burberry's desired consumer – the young and the hip – but significantly more working-class consumers?

This influx of less well-off customers drove the production of imitation goods, and the spectre of fakes came back to haunt Burberry once again. However, these fakes were not merely straightforward copies of Nova check scarves and hats, but specially produced items where the counterfeiters had effectively changed the silhouette to a baggy hooded top and a tracksuit bottom, products that Burberry did not design or produce. This new consumer demographic at Burberry threw up a paradox for the company, and while using luxury brands as a way of 'passing' or boosting cultural capital on a local level is easily understood, this did not apply to 'chav' culture. Burberry attempted to distance itself from 'chav' culture by limiting the quantity of Nova check on its products and by shelving production of the baseball caps, however this only served to make those products scarce and therefore highly sought after, creating what May and Sell (2005) describe as a rivalrous state. Product scarcity also drove many consumers to websites selling counterfeit clothing and accessories, which had the potential to damage Burberry's brand value as two key assets, the Burberry Nova check and the Equestrian Knight logo, were commonly used in fakes, and as Moor points out, since the 1980s, there has been a growing recognition of the 'brand as asset' (2007: 91) therefore any disruption to the brand had the potential to directly impact its revenue stream.

Burberry's history within marginal youth cultures stretches back to the mid-1960s, and has strong connections with Mod culture, a primarily masculine community, and we saw how this sense of masculinity runs through other sub-cultures with a connection to Burberry, including football hooligans where a gender divide was present. And while men used Burberry to stand out, to be respected – even if that was to be feared – women used it as what Partington (1992) describes as a means of social betterment. However, white working-class women were taken to task for misappropriating Burberry and they became targets for accusations of tastelessness. Even in 2008, negative brand associations still surrounded Burberry, and a sense of ignominy was directed at women, as this invective editorial in *The Times* shows: 'The clever but naïve idea to print a few affordable Burberry headscarves and bikinis to rid itself of its stuffy image turned into a highly contagious virus' (Olins, 2008). The linguistic style of this piece suggests enragement with the brand; however it is only women's wear that has been singled out. Despite Olins's editorial, the brand was largely found not to be at fault, and the British press and media continued to turn on customers who were viewed as 'misusing' the brand. Those consumers were subsequently used as a cautionary tale to other luxury companies through the spread of hate speech, particularly in relation to the female 'celebrity chav'. Social media helped some consumers to fight back against a mainstream view of the 'bad' consumer, however we saw how their conflict, while boosting cultural capital momentarily on a local level, ultimately did not impact dominant culture's view on a permanent basis.

Ultimately, this chapter underlines how Bravo's attention to age, not class, underestimated the impact of the lower cost lines and that the legacy of her decision to expand Burberry's product range to include bikinis and baseball caps led to a divergence in brand perception, and to complications of consumption. However, Burberry has been relatively unscathed financially by its proximity to 'bad' consumers, and the storm surrounding them proved to be an isolated and a particularly British one.

In the next chapter, Burberry's mixed messages in terms of UK consumer recognition continues, and the closure of their production plant in Treorchy in 2007 is the primary focus. The chapter also investigates the importance of place and origin in terms of fashion production, and how this proved both straightforward and problematic for the brand.

5

The £13,000 handbag

In March 2007, a clothing production plant in the small Welsh town of Treorchy closed its doors for the last time. The factory was owned and run by luxury fashion brand Burberry, and they made a decision to move a large part of their production to factories outside the UK. The Burberry Annual Report for 2006–07 reveals that total revenue for the year showed an increase of 15 per cent, taking it to £850.3 million, and directors proposed a 31 per cent increase to shareholders in their year-end dividends. Though still not a giant in fashion revenue terms, Burberry was making a healthy profit. The Treorchy plant solely produced men's polo shirts, and Burberry found that by moving production from Wales to countries including China they could significantly reduce unit costs. This became one of the major causes of grievance amongst the workforce at Treorchy when they heard the news about their job losses: they simply could not understand why a profitable plant would be closed down, especially given its long and illustrious history in the town.

The factory was built in the 1930s, and had become a familiar part of the town's infrastructure, and through it Treorchy had developed a long and proud history of working with fashion, fabrics and apparel. At its peak in the 1960s, the factory employed close to 1,500 people, mainly women from the local area, and at the time of the closure it employed over 300 people, and was considered a significant local employer. This part of the Rhondda was designated as a special development area by the British Government in the 1930s, due to the loss of jobs in the declining local mining industry. Long-term unemployment had been endemic in the area from the 1930s, and the pattern continued throughout the following decades up to the miner's strike in the 1980s, when the collieries were finally closed.

The loss of full-time jobs at the Burberry plant was a huge cause for concern in a town with a population of 2,000, as it would leave a sizable economic chasm. The history of the town with its skilled and dedicated workforce created a complex economic, commercial and social backdrop to the industrial action that took place in the winter of 2006–07: this action involved not just employees and their unions, but Local and Central Government, the Welsh Assembly, the European Parliament, national and international press media, Burberry customers in the UK, United States and in Europe, and friends, families and celebrities in support of the workforce. The struggle to keep the plant open became a regular national news item during February and March 2007, and some of the workforce became reluctant 'celebrities' because of their involvement in the campaign.

In order to understand why the closure of this particular plant caused such public interest, and why the ensuing struggle became a newsworthy, and largely popular narrative, I examined it through two contrasting studies: Blyton and Jenkins's (2012) 'Mobilizing Resistance: The Burberry Workers' Campaign Against Factory Closure' and through an oral history project of my own – 'Can Craft Make You Happy?' (2009) where I talked to a small group of women who had lost their jobs at the plant. Both studies examine the closure of the long-established production plant, and use informal interviews with the workforce, however the differentiation between each study begins with the methodological approach, and ends with a variation in conclusion: Mobilizing Resistance talks up the success of the campaign, while Can Craft Make You Happy? draws a less optimistic conclusion.

Mobilizing Resistance

The focus of Blyton and Jenkins study is largely on the bitter negotiations in the lead up to the closure, and the spectacle of the protest campaign prior to the closedown. Blyton and Jenkins draw on frame analysis to show how what they describe as a benign workforce were professionally mobilized and came to act collectively when they had shown little or no desire to do so in the past. Their overall analysis acknowledges the journey taken by the Treorchy workforce, who moved from their previously passive position to a more activist and collective role, and how this went against sector norms. It is unsurprising that Blyton and Jenkins were interested in investigating how this workforce were able to act collectively, and that their activism went against the majority of industrial disputes in the UK, particularly in the garment production sector where they describe an almost total lack of action, and this forms the backbone of their good news story. Of course there was much to celebrate during the lengthy and bitter campaign where the workforce fought a fierce battle to save their plant, and where they 'campaigned around corporate greed, applied a moral and ethical critique to globalization, and held an international clothing brand up to public censure for its treatment not only of its employees, but also its customers' (2012: 26). Mobilizing Resistance highlights the importance of perceived substantive and procedural injustice among the workforce, and how the geographic location and community characteristics strengthened their resolve to fight the closure. These issues form the core of their study and Blyton and Jenkins show how the workforce were moved along a path of interconnected frames, from summarizing, to organizing, to rationalizing and ending in what they call the injustice frame. The study follows the workforce along their journey, describing the campaign as it happened, using the words of those involved. Mobilizing Resistance builds an image of the workforce, starting the moment they hear the entire plant is to be closed, throughout the campaign, and up to the last day of action.

The study begins with a description of the workforce that helps to contextualize their starting point, and demonstrate how unusual their collective action was, and how it differed from other workers in the garment sector. At the outset of the study Blyton and Jenkins refer to the workforce as individualistic, but cooperative, willing and able to work with their employer in very flexible ways. Burberry dominated the local employment market so employees tended to comply with their management, and many families had multiple ties with the factory, and helped to recruit other family members – male and female, across multiple generations. As one respondent put it 'we used to say "you were right for life" [at Burberry]', indicating that Burberry was seen as a refuge from the increasingly casualized local labour market. Despite grumbles about low rates of pay, particularly amongst the machinists, there was very little industrial action at the plant. Blyton and Jenkins note that 'resistance has tended to be individualized and unorganized, mainly in the form of absence' (2012: 30).

Mobilizing Resistance reports that during negotiations in 2004 – two years before the announcement of the closure, a new plant manager was appointed and productivity rose by over 20 per cent, signalling an increase in machinists wages of 6 per cent, though Blyton and Jenkins state that they 'remained dissatisfied with their earnings. Garment workers are generally low paid, but for some years, the Treorchy machinists had experienced a steady erosion of their piecework incentives by the advance of the National Minimum Wage' (2012: 33). This issue had been a source of grievance for some time, and there had been no effective organization around it, which reflected sector norm and this particular workforce's reputation for compliance. The study pinpoints two key elements that initiated a change of heart within the workforce, and a hardening of attitude towards their employers, one of which was the reduction of product mix at the plant, where they solely produced men's polo shirts. The second element, which hit the workforce even harder, was that this very lack of product diversity became one of the reasons Burberry used to rationalize the closure. Blyton and Jenkins show how Burberry used this 'one product' excuse as a reason to continue with their plans for closure.

> A further element in the attribution of blame and defining of injustice was to emerge a short way into the campaign, when, under pressure to justify their actions and the decision to close the plant rather than change its product mix, senior Burberry mangers cited a 'lack of skills' at the plant which precluded assigning alternative garments in order to stave off closure. (2012: 35–6)

The study describes the feelings of hurt emanating from the workforce, and how their pride and self-image had been damaged. They reported the comments of one long-serving worker: 'We made everything at that factory … we could do every job there was' (2012: 36). However, the ultimate call to arms came with the single most important element in the entire winding-down campaign: a mishandling of the closure announcement. *Mobilising Resistance* details the event noting that Burberry hired private security to surround the plant at Treorchy while severance notices were printed out for the entire workforce. An executive from Burberry went unheard as she shouted instructions over the noise of the plant machinery, which was left running throughout the first part of her announcement. Blyton and Jenkins report that some of the Burberry executives were seen on the factory floor immediately after the announcement, talking on their mobile phones, smiling and laughing, which the workforce regarded as symptomatic of their disregard for their feelings. The study details the way the Notice of Closure was announced and how it provided a clear focus for the workforce, drawing them closer to what Blyton and Jenkins refer to as *an embattled 'us'*, where the formerly benevolent view of their employer was shattered forever. There was a strong sense of injustice, as the workforce had kept their side of the bargain and fulfilled their production quotas, yet had not succeeded in keeping their jobs. Blyton and Jenkins cite the appointment of the new plant manager in 2004 as another key element in the closure, but show how changes in the organization were viewed as positive strategies by the workforce. Similarly, negotiations with plant unions, the GMB (Britain's General Union) and Amicus, emphasized the need to achieve increases in productivity as a means of ensuring the continuing secure status of the plant. Blyton and Jenkins place a strong sense of localism at the centre of the struggle citing the abrupt departure of the previous plant manager as the moment the future of the factory was sealed. They report several workers saying: '[We think] he … was got rid of because he would have fought tooth and nail for this factory. He was from the Rhondda, and he would have made it awkward for them [Burberry HQ]' (2012: 35).

Public interest in the struggle was still some way off, but Mobilizing Resistance shows how the anti-closure campaign captured a wider demographic by placing the Burberry consumer alongside the workforce, pointing out that '[this] had wider social appeal than what might otherwise have been regarded as workers' narrow economistic self-interest in preserving their jobs' (2012: 38). The study points out that consumers had started to ask some difficult questions of the brand, including why they were still paying premium prices for goods produced in low-cost plants, where the workforce were paid less and worked without union support. Despite all the public and political support, the factory closed, and Blyton and Jenkins attribute the closure to a wide range of elements, including poor leadership skills amongst full-time union representatives, who not only failed to secure GMB membership at the remaining two UK-based Burberry plants to show solidarity, but who also did not capitalize sufficiently on the political support they received from Parliament and the Welsh Assembly, and that the campaign to save the plant remained 'largely at the micro, workplace level' (2012: 41).

Mobilizing Resistance concludes soon after the campaign comes to a close, and Blyton and Jenkins clearly summarize what they consider successful elements of the campaign, including how a tipping point of injustice brought an individualized workforce together to act collectively; that the GMB and Amicus did not focus entirely on pay and conditions for the workforce, but broadened the debate to include customers, and how successful negotiations by the unions achieved higher levels of severance pay, however, their principal success story was that the mainly female workforce went against the social norms of this sector, and battled to save their jobs, believing they had little to lose.

Can Craft Make You Happy?

I used my background as a contemporary visual art curator with specialist skills in fashion and textiles to develop 'Can Craft Make You Happy?', which was financially supported through the Crafts Council's Spark Plug curatorial award scheme. This helped to fund a primary research programme with a small group of women who were made redundant when the plant was closed. In the study,

I describe how the women reacted to the closure, and detail images of their lives post-closure. I was interested to understand what it was like to work, to make a livelihood at the Burberry plant at Treorchy and how it felt after the company was no longer part of their lives. We developed a dialogue that explored their experiences, stories, ethical codes, social fabric and friendships that helped to create a vivid image of their time at the factory. I was also interested to see what had provoked them into action, and if they were indeed what Blyton and Jenkins (2012) termed passive. I talked to the women about their early career experiences of marking out with patterns and chalk and cutting with oversized shears, and what it was like to handle fine fabrics that make luxury clothing and apparel. I was also interested to know what it was like to make a winter coat that retailed at this time for more than £800, when take home pay was set at £5.25 per hour, the adult minimum wage level in 2006, essentially making the workforce part of the luxury fashion sector, but unable to be a consumer of it. Equally, I was interested to know how their workplace experience moved from an initial source of pride, to feelings of anger and resentment and how their long history of producing clothes for the luxury market impacted their feelings when it ceased to be a part of their lives. Ultimately, I wanted to know if an important Burberry trademark, the (in)famous Nova check had become an agent of change that forced the women concerned to confront their worst fears, and whether the cloth itself had become toxic.

In order to develop and deliver Can Craft Make You Happy? I visited the Rhondda town of Treorchy on six occasions between 2008 and 2009. The first time was as a guest of the GMB (the largest trade union at the plant) at a reunion marking the one-year anniversary of the closure. GMB Wales had organized anti-closure protest campaigns in London, Cardiff and Treorchy, so I contacted them directly and spoke to Mervyn Burnett, the full-time GMB officer responsible for orchestrating the main campaigns. Burnett's name had cropped up in the press and was on the GMB site, and when we spoke, I asked about the welfare of the women who had been made redundant, and he asked me about my research and invited me to the reunion in Treorchy. The GMB also extended an open invitation to their offices in Cardiff, and I was given unlimited access to press materials from the campaign. When I attended the reunion, Burnett introduced me to Joan Young, a former machinist and shop steward at the plant. I was also introduced to the Welsh Assembly Member for Rhondda, the Managing Director of Talk HR Solutions in Pontypool and the Engagement Gateway Development Officer from voluntary sector organization, Interlink. This visit gave me the opportunity to gather invaluable primary research materials, as I was able to talk to an ex-employee, a union official, employment and training experts and an elected politician. Though these voices were pre-selected by GMB Wales, the union nonetheless provided a gateway that opened up a privileged access to some of the key people and organizations that took part in the struggle to keep the Burberry plant open.

I worked closely with Joan Young, and used word-of-mouth recommendations to approach former Burberry employees in order to talk about the turbulent times during the run up to the closure. My sample group was small, but adopting an oral history approach was fruitful as the women showed a warm, humorous and inclusive side to their lives, and their stories reflected their social cohesion.

Meeting Joan Young

My first visit to Treorchy in March 2008 was to attend the one-year reunion of the closure. It was a noisy affair, so Joan offered to meet me the following day to show me around some significant locations in the town. The whole weekend in Treorchy was wild and windy, and it rained hard for the two days I was there, which further added to my impression of the town being physically and metaphorically swept away. Joan met me at the train station in Ynyswen – a tiny neighbouring station close to Treorchy. She was in a little car and we started on our journey, but my chance to look at the sites was considerably hampered as I had to roll down the passenger window as we approached a significant site, and roll it up again swiftly afterwards, before we both got soaking wet, however it was important to Joan that I saw these sites. The journey she took followed the route of the march she and her co-workers took on the final day of the plant – what some media coverage described as The Victory March. Joan showed me where they had set off, which gate they had used, who she was walking with, who else was present, what banner they carried, where they stopped en route, who spoke to the television crews, what they said, which station they spoke to and what country they came from; she described the jazz band, and the choir, the guest speakers and the well-wishers lining the streets. We went from the factory site in the centre of the town, passed through the narrow developments of nineteenth-century houses, to the Parc and Dare – the building they used for a last-ditch public meeting – and Joan described what that building meant to her and what it meant to the town. We examined history, politics, commerce, gender, socialization and hierarchy. Joan's stories breathed life into the streets and homes and businesses of this small Welsh town. She told me that she felt like an ordinary person, yet her exhaustive commentary suggested otherwise, and that she had been forever changed and politicized by the events leading up to the closure. The act of witnessing this monumental struggle had taken over her life, and the retelling of stories about the GMB, the factory and her ex-colleagues, suggests that this narrative may never be fully put to rest, as Joan relives these events over and over, she tries to reconcile or even make right what has happened to her and her colleagues.

Part of my study focused on working with fabrics at the factory, which helped to give me a temporal and historical context to the job losses. When Joan started at the factory in the 1960s, other types of employment on offer in the area, particularly for young woman, were very limited. There was retail and catering work in Treorchy, which was unskilled and offered few opportunities for career development, and only Harwin Components, an electronics company, offered work to women and girls mainly in the offices, which meant that securing a job at Burberry was aspirational, and Joan describes how from an early age, she knew what she wanted 'hand sewer I wanted to be. Hand sewer'. These longed-for jobs, and long history of clothing production made losing their employment all the more poignant, as many of the women I spoke to had spent almost their entire working lives at Burberry. Another woman who started work at the factory in the mid-1960s was Anne, who, influenced by her mother, who was a dressmaker, had also wanted to work with fabrics and fashion for most of her life. Anne started work at the factory aged 15 after her aunt, who was a hand sewer at the plant, recommended her for a job. Joan was sixteen and secured a job after her sister 'put in a good word' with the manager. As Anne puts it 'If your mother or sister worked there, you were taken seriously.' Both women worked at the plant for over forty years, and reasonably expected to spend the remainder of their working years there. When Joan and Anne started, the factory was run by sister company Polikoff, who shared production facilities with Burberry at their London site in Chatham Place, Hackney. Polikoff became part of the Great Universal Stores conglomerate, who took over the plant in 1955, and initially both women produced officer uniforms for the Army and the RAF, made from luxurious wools and silks. They subsequently produced many other luxury lines including wool and cashmere coats, duffels, trench coats, casual jackets, quilted jackets and suits, and all employees needed a high level of skill and a lot of experience to construct this kind of clothing. Anne recalled undergoing a six-week in-house training course when she started at the plant, however this level of high-quality training is almost completely absent in the current employment landscape, a fact supported by findings in the Treorchy Social Audit (Adamson and Byrne, 2008) who underlined the lack of local opportunities.

Both Anne and Joan remember cutting and sewing luxury fabrics, and though they were both experienced seamstresses, they still remember the agony of making a mistake, where they would have to report to the manager to ask for more fabric. Here, they were shouted at and reminded in no uncertain terms that they were working 'on an £800 coat'. Anne remembers being so absorbed by her work that she noticed the way every garment was produced, even one day while sitting on a bus she noticed 'a woman wearing a Burberry coat and the collar wasn't sewn quite correctly'. Injuries at work were common and all the women I spoke to reported regular accidents, with burns being the most common incident, followed by repetitive strain injury caused by wielding heavy scissors. Joan complained about a job she was given matching checks on a run of expensive coats 'on the hood, the yoke, the pockets, all matching. The worst job I ever had'. It severely affected her eyesight and caused carpel tunnel syndrome. All the women I spoke to suffered from ganglia after pressing down pattern pieces with the full span of their hand, as there were no mechanized cutting facilities at the plant in the 1960s, so each garment was cut out by hand.

All of my research was conducted with women, and mainly older women, and they point out that there were big differences in what their employer viewed as skilled and unskilled labour, which created a clear gender divide. However, one of the biggest changes to male and female employment occurred after Burberry became a publicly listed company in 2002, and Anne told me that in the final years of the factory men occupied *all* the positions in the cutting room and on the presses, and that they 'they earned twice as much as the 'girls'. However, the women agreed that the men in the pressing room offered them a good deal, as they pressed clothes – suits, coats etc. – brought in from home, for 20p per item, the proceeds of which were given to charity. This narrative was repeatedly talked-up by the women as an act of charity, and was used as a way of displacing the disparity in wages. In the years after 2002, Joan recalled that when the work was slow, caused by a delivery delay or hold up in production, rather than utilizing her extensive skillset, she was asked to do some very basic tasks. 'If you didn't have nothing to do, they put you on spare buttons. 100 counted out, and one per bag.'

The old mechanized equipment from Polikoff's had been replaced with technologically advanced machinery when Burberry took over the plant in 1989, and it was this element that divided the genders, splitting them into skilled and unskilled, as it's hard to argue that counting buttons or sorting swing tags calls for either skill or experience, only endurance. Other differences in work practice under Polikoff's and Burberry included an economic competitiveness amongst the workforce, as the women aimed for some sort of parity. The women I spoke to recalled that in their early days at the factory, they all found creative ways of boosting their wage packets by beating the timings and minutes, which they learned informally on the job by watching the older women. Anne described one woman who worked at the factory when she first started: 'One old lady used to take her tin home at night and thread her needles ready.' At Polikoff's all women aged eighteen and over earned full pay, however Joan reports that as a sixteen-year-old, she was earning as much as an adult as she was so quick, making up her wages by achieving bonus targets, but by the time the Burberry plant closed, the average adult wage was just £208.00 per week. Other non-monetary bonuses were lost when Burberry became a listed company, and incentives in the form of the highly anticipated Christmas raffle, where workers had the chance of winning a television, a camera or a hamper of food were suspended and replaced with gift certificates to spend in the on-site Burberry shop. Other perks, including mail-order catalogues brought in to make extra income from colleagues were banned from the workplace, as management thought they encouraged people to chat, and diverted them from their work. Inexplicably, given the reasons for the original confiscation, each employee was given a copy of the *Kay's* catalogue, owned and controlled by Burberry's parent company at the time, Great Universal Stores. This chipping away of remuneration and reward in the workplace formed the background, and added considerable volume to the eventual industrial action that took place in the Autumn and Winter of 2006–7.

Production mix reduced

One of the most contentious times at the Treorchy plant concerns Burberry's decision to cut production down to just one garment – the men's polo shirt – and it is difficult to gauge the level of humiliation amongst the workforce, and how deeply this hurt them. Given the enormous pride in their craft skills, and years of working with fine fabrics, to suddenly find themselves in charge of producing part of a polo shirt felt in many ways like a punishment, as Joan argues 'when they bring it down to only one product, that's a slippery slope'. Leigh was one of the youngest women I spent time with, and she voiced her concerns when the factory was only producing men's polo shirts 'you know, but then we all said, oh, all our eggs in one basket'. Leigh lamented the gradual loss of product mix, and in her final years at the factory she worked in the supply stores. She had worked at the plant since she was sixteen, and so had a long history with Burberry, and she recalled the diversity of work and the sheer volume of production: 'We had a raincoat section, trouser section, jacket section; they had the Army section, and gradually the Army went, the raincoats went, there was just the duffle coats, then it turned all over then the polo shirts, and then closure.'

The consequences of Burberry's decision to cut the product mix at the Treorchy plant seemed to shock the company and opened them up to scrutiny and criticism from UK and international press and media. Observer journalist Carole Cadwalladr reported comments made by a Burberry spokesman suggesting 'bemusement' at the degree of media coverage for the protests as 'perverse … for a polo-shirt factory' (2007: 36). The backlash against Burberry heightened as the company didn't signal any kind of compassion for the workforce, and their fairness as an employer was called into question, not only by the workforce, but also by its customers. However, the biggest casualty was the Burberry workforce, who had been stripped of their product mix rendering their skills base, their experience and their ingenuity redundant. The women I talked to commented on how remote the local management had become, however they were aware of a change at the very top of the organizational structure: the appointment of a new CEO, Angela Ahrendts, who had made herself visible to the workforce when she issued a little notebook to all employees one Christmas.

Joan   'When that woman started up in London, we all had the
           notebook …'
Leigh 'Ah, yes, the notebook.'
Joan   'And within 12 months we were all made redundant.'

Ahrendts sent a directive that each employee was to be given a notebook containing a short history of the company. This seemed a curious move by Burberry, as it could be argued that the workforce knew more about its history than a newly appointed Chief Executive Officer whose previous work had included tenures at Donna Karen, Liz Claiborne and Juicy Couture. The 'notebook' incident marked another deflating episode for the women I spoke to, and in retrospect it provided a key visual reminder of the downward spiral they were now entering.

The Notice of Closure announcement in September 2006

Two years after the stripped-back product mix at the Burberry plant, came the almost inevitable Notice of Closure. Joan remembers the day vividly, and how her advice to the Burberry executives, dispatched from head office to summarily give notice to the entire workforce, went unheeded.

> We – we were in work and they called for myself and John Harris to go up to the office. Every time the union was called up there, 'Oh they're shutting the place, they're shutting the place' they said, isn't it? So up we went, this was about half past nine and we were taken into a room I hadn't been in before, and then the – one of the directors came in and said they were down from London.
>
> And they came in and said they were closing the place. I said 'Oh, how am I going to go down there and tell them that now?' And she said, 'You don't have to, I will now'. So I said 'Are you going to let them have their breakfast first?' 'No, I'll have to tell them now because they can't be sent home without this letter.'
>
> But she wouldn't wait, anyway, she went and said it, when you look back now she should have waited for the two breaks, cleared the canteen out, had everyone in there, but all she did was stand on a box at the top of the factory and called everybody round, they couldn't hear what she was saying, they had to put the main electricity power off 'cause there was just "mmmm" like that, hard to be heard and people were saying "What's she saying like, what's she – what is she saying?"'

The plant was surrounded by security men hired by Burberry, and the workforce were not allowed to leave the site until they had been given their written notice, which were being printed out, very slowly, in the management offices. Leigh recalls the moment she heard the news about the closure, and saw many of the women go into shock.

> Yes, yes, we were there, this announcement came over that we all had to meet at a certain area in the factory, which we did, and she just stood over a little box and told us we were finishing. It was – well some people was crying, the younger ones. I was deeply shocked but not crying, some of the older ones were crying, you know, some of the people had been there all their lives. Well, I – really I'd been there all my life, I know I got started at 16, you know, so – but there were people who'd been there 30, 40 years, you know.
>
> But --, well I was --, nobody did any work then, it was, you know, everybody was shocked.

I think we knew there was something up because there was so many suits in, in the morning, we thought, oh you know. I did think perhaps 50, 60 people made redundant, something like that, you know.

But when they actually came round and said everything was going, well I think everybody in the factory was really shocked, I really do. So we just stood around, we weren't allowed out of the factory, we couldn't – couldn't leave, we had security on the gate and everyone was sitting round in little huddles not knowing what to do.

The nature of fairness cropped up again and again, not only within the workforce, but also on a broader, more international basis where customers examined exactly what they were buying. Why, they asked, were they paying a high price for luxury clothes and accessories produced cheaply in international factories? This question contributed to a significant change in the way Burberry was viewed, and became a turning point where consumers had a chance to become citizens, with rights to boycott goods and services that failed to meet their expectations. This single issue – where consumers became involved in collective action – marked a distinction between the plight of the Burberry workers, and that of other workers involved in labour disputes. The GMB designed a high-profile campaign, and at events that took place outside Burberry's national and international flagship stores, consumers were vocal about the Treorchy plant closure. The action outside the Bond Street store in London's Mayfair attracted a lot of media attention, and Joan – who was present at this protest, remembers the day in February 2007 when she was surrounded by international press media.

'Will you do an interview with me now?' 'Yes', and another one was telling her 'I want her first.' Well you've never seen the like, you haven't. So many camera crews were there, wanting to speak to you, isn't it?

Joan and her colleagues had never taken part in any kind of protest, but now found themselves involved in subterfuge, which Joan thought was both thrilling and hilarious. 'They went in [to the Bond Street store] and bought a shirt and then cut it in half outside. My scissors, I was keeping them hidden because we shouldn't be out with scissors, so I kept them well hidden in my handbag.' One of the men went into the store with a gift certificate, and Joan remembers that as they were cutting the shirt 'he went in with his £30 worth of vouchers, and for thirty pounds all he could get was a scrunchie for your hair, and he hasn't got a hair on his head, which was a laugh'.

The media focused on Burberry's decision to move production away from Wales and into China, Portugal, Poland and Spain – all countries with lower labour costs – however the GMB and the Burberry workers did not want to scapegoat these new employees within their campaign: they wanted to show solidarity for their fellow workers, despite differences in pay scale and working conditions. At the height of the campaign Burberry was scrutinized by customers, press and media, shareholders, financiers, politicians and its competitors in the UK and abroad. Actors Ioan Gruffudd and Rachel Weisz, who both worked as models for the company at this time added their voices to the anti-closure campaign, and this opened the door to further criticism about the company and the media spotlight made public the largely invisible workforce behind the brand.

Not everyone in Treorchy and the surrounding Rhondda Valley shared a sense of outrage about the closure, and when I first visited the town in 2008, I travelled by taxi to the reunion, which was hosted at the local football club. On my way there, the cab driver asked me what I was doing in the Valleys, and became infuriated when I told him I was writing about the Burberry women. He argued that there was 'far too much emphasis' placed on that site. He regarded the Burberry wages as pin money, and not a real wage with any proper economic power, which was a fair appraisal in terms of the women's take-home pay. He had been made redundant years earlier, and it was clear that he felt overlooked, his anger went unnoticed and had become displaced and his feelings seemed to reflect what Ahmed (2010) describes as spoiling the norm. However, there was a chance that after years of deferring to fathers and husbands, the women's apparent change in behaviour perhaps now came across as joyless, and indeed they may have been in danger of becoming outsiders in a community where they had forever been on the inside. The lack of empathy for the Burberry workers was not solely isolated to men, and on the BBC Wales comments pages in March 2007, Susan Carlick, a former GMB works convenor, wrote about the closure of the local Rizla plant in nearby Treforest in 2005. She was understandably very bitter, and references her highly skilled workforce, and how vital it was to keep jobs in the Valley, whether skilled or unskilled, but fails to understand the differences between Burberry and the Rizla brand. Burberry trade on their 'Made in Britain' heritage and status, which lends the brand what Pike (2010) describes as a geographic entanglement to the UK, and also, by widening the campaign to include more than just pay and conditions for the Treorchy employees, the GMB were able to attract consumer interest to their cause. By involving consumers within the protests, where they marched side-by-side with the workforce, the GMB were able to use this expanded focus to make a bespoke and inclusive plan to keep production British, and they were also able to use one of Burberry's key selling points in their fight.

After the closure

When I caught up with the women in 2009, they told me about their on-going search for work. Leigh had been more successful than most, securing a new job at a chemist in Treorchy. She worked part-time, so her take home pay was substantially less than her Burberry wages, however she felt fortunate that she was still working locally. Two of Leigh's former colleagues had secured work making duvet covers in Merthyr Tydfil, and another had set up her own clothing alteration business, but these were very rare exceptions. Joan, like many other ex-Burberry employees, had a new job as a care assistant. 'Pauline, Elaine, Diane, Claire, and Susan, all work at Ty Ross.' Ty Ross is a local care home, and one of the few employers in the area offering any kind of work. The work on offer was unpopular, as the hours were long and irregular, and the shift patterns involved working unsocial hours – at night, at the weekend, at Christmas and New Year. During the first winter after the Burberry closure, Joan had to work on Christmas day, and got into trouble with her employer as her husband kept phoning to check how to cook the dinner as he was inexperienced in the kitchen. Joan was very unhappy that at nearly sixty years old she had been forced to work on Christmas day for the very first time, but also that the social roles between her and her husband were skewed. Shortly after this incident, Joan suffered an injury at work, and subsequently tried to find a new job that involved less lifting. She responded to an advert looking for shop assistants in a nearby town:

> *I've been down to Pontypridd asking for two jobs in boutiques. The one, they said 'put your name and address, and your age on here', and the two in front of me – they were 17 and 18. But you don't know what they're looking for. They said they wanted a mature person.*
>
> *In the other shop he said 'I've got a young range of wear, and I need someone more in the range of, you know.*

Though employment legislation forbids using age as a barrier, in practice it may be widespread and unchallenged. For some former Burberry employees, there was a ray of hope when a small branch of Asda opened in the town just after the closure of the plant. A handful of ex-employees were given jobs there, however as the store did not meet profit expectations, they were all laid off again not long after it opened. When a town with a population of 2,000 loses over 300 full-time jobs, and those who are working have low levels of income and uneven earning patterns, blame was attributed to the fact that there simply wasn't enough money in the local economy to keep the shop afloat. Contradictorily, the Treorchy Social Audit reports a net increase of employment rates in the area, however the majority were low skilled and low paid. The skilled and stable jobs seemed to be long gone, but the Audit states that this increase 'generally obscures a continual process of turnover in the local employment base in which particular firms shed jobs or close down even as new firms start operating in the area. The local perception is that these losses have primarily occurred in the more established (and better paying) factories, some of which have recently shed jobs or moved out of the area altogether. Examples of this included recent redundancies at the Burberrys factory and the closure of Harwins components' (Adamson and Byrne, 2008: 2.5). The Treorchy Audit reveals the level of fear the closure had on the town, and how whole families were at risk of becoming work-poor households, where some may never work again. All the women I talked to discussed the family referral system, and they felt that this had come back to haunt them now they had all lost their jobs. Joan shared her newspaper clippings, showing me a photograph of a family who lost their jobs 'all of them, look – mother, father and son worked in the factory'. The Treorchy Audit shows evidence that declining unemployment had not been evenly distributed and that unemployment continued to be concentrated within households where no one is in employment. The Audit also shows that the lack of skilled and well-paid work in the area was a source of despondency, and that young people 'see their parents in low paid employment and they see no hope'. Former Burberry machinist Anne told me 'my niece, she's coming up 18 and she hadn't had a job yet'. One interviewee in the Treorchy Audit suggests that as wages were so low in the local labour market, this has added a push-out factor to work outside the area, whether as a daily commuter, or on a more permanent basis. The women I talked to started work at 7.45 in the morning, but worked locally so didn't have to travel far, however they all noted that where there were jobs, they were often located miles away involving long journeys on public transport. Several of Joan's former work mates were employed in a care home in Llantresant, a commute involving two bus rides, which is a significant journey in a rural area.

Though the women spoke fondly about the majority of their time at Polikoff and Burberry, they noticed a regime change when Burberry formally took over in 1989. Anne remembers Polikoff's as 'very family oriented', and the company allowed parents to tend to sick children, and attend to other caring responsibilities and family emergencies. Burberry, by contrast, were thought of as inflexible employers. Anne remembered a time when her son was involved in a road traffic accident and had been taken to hospital. She had to wait in order to receive a permission slip to leave the factory, and the clerk tried to persuade her to 'go another day' as it was inconvenient at that time. However, despite this style of management, there was a discernible sense of community emanating from the women I spoke to, one in which more vulnerable members of the workforce were supported by their workmates. As Joan remarked: 'It's a proper community, one where people look after one another.' The women told me of a former colleague who had been suspended from work for selling Burberry polo shirts at a local golf club. He'd bought the shirts from the onsite shop, and was shocked at his suspension. The women had a whip round for him, and gave their cash freely to support him and his family when his wages were docked. Joan told me that her reason for standing as a union representative was to 'look after the underdog' and this sense of responsibility runs deep through their collective psyche. The women talked about workmates with disabilities and how they supported them, including one man with learning differences. 'The men would tease him, but the women wouldn't have it. They stood up for him.' I asked where he was now the factory had closed.

> He hadn't got a job. He's walking the streets, um … first of all with his sister's dog, didn't he? But they had him put down, or something. He hasn't got a new one now so he walks by himself. His mother used to say 'he walked the dog to death.' He walks for miles and miles.
>
> You go to say 'Hiya Dave, how are you?' but all you can say is 'Hiya Dave' and he answers 'I'm alright thank you' quick as a flash, because he knows that's what you were going to ask.

The women talked about the informal support structure around him at the factory, where his manager told him exactly what he needed to do, patiently, task by task, maintaining personal contact with him throughout the day. A space was found at the factory so that he could work and be useful and needed. When the factory closed, he found, like many others, that he was no longer useful or needed and he quickly spiralled into difficulty, as there was no formal structure in place to support him. Many former employees have suffered from ill health since the closure, with depression, dementia and alcoholism topping the list. One former colleague of Joan and Anne's lapsed into alcoholism and ran up debts on his rent and bills, and was entering his property by climbing through the bathroom window, as the bailiffs had locked all the doors. As Joan says 'people used to look out for him'. These acts of kindness fall outside a formal system, and as Skeggs (1997) argues, domestic labour in the form of the 'care system' have become quantifiable and calculative, but these acts of generosity, what can be described as giving outside the contract, are un-quantifiable and incalculable acts of kindness.

One of the biggest and largely unseen consequences of the closure was the loss of important social structures, particularly those built up at work, but which were rarely acted on outside working hours. Most of the women I spoke to did not socialize with work colleagues, but built up networks during working hours, often sustaining very long friendships. I came to understand that their social lives did not mirror my own, and that this generation of women put their families first, and friendship was for work hours. All the women say they still see old workmates in the street or at the shop, but as Leigh recalled, it's rarely to say more than 'are you working yet? as we rush past one another'.

My primary research showed that their social networks were no longer intact, and so when I caught up with the women in 2009, they had not seen one another for months. I found that their resentment towards Burberry was undiminished, they have a heightened awareness of the Burberry profit margin, and the fact that the Treorchy plant made a lot of money for the company still hurts them. One factor that compromises their feelings towards Burberry are the gifts the company used to give to them each Christmas, and where once they cherished the products and made presents of the handbags, umbrellas and shirts to daughters, mothers and husbands, now they are repelled. As Leigh asked 'I wouldn't wear Burberry now, would you Joan?'

> *No, I would not. Mike had a shirt and he'd wear it at the caravan, but now when he puts it on, you just think (shudders) oh, no. And the girls* (Joan's two daughters) *don't use their handbags any more, no.*

The Burberry trademark Nova check has become toxic to the women, yet a strong sense of thrift still runs its course, which meant that the women could not throw anything away. As Anne remarks 'we had these gifts at Christmas time, see. There's a Burberry umbrella under the stairs'.

> Leigh *'I have a lot of stuff under the stairs too'*
> Joan *'I have a walking stick upstairs, brand new, and none of the girls wanted it.'*
> Leigh *'I won't throw it out, mind.'*

A sense of pride is bound up in the products, and where once they were proud that they were able to give family members a luxury item with the easily identifiable Nova check, now they recoil in horror from this pattern. Leigh talked about Cardiff City fans publicly dumping their unofficial Burberry 'uniform' after the closure, stating that in the past 'you wouldn't see a Cardiff City shirt, you'd see a Burberry shirt'. The *Connaught*, famous for being the nearest pub to the Cardiff City ground at Ninian Park, and for banning anyone wearing Burberry, is now free of this aesthetic.

Burberry's Trust Fund

Joan and former colleague Gaynor were involved in distributing funds from the Trust Fund set up by Burberry in the aftermath of the closure. Both women were proud to represent the workforce and make decisions on what to fund and to what level, however the amounts they have disbursed so far are small, and the requests are slow to arrive. Joan and Gaynor worked with Mervyn Burnett, Chris Bryant MP and Leighton Andrews AM, and they have funded a small range of requests, ranging from an HGV license to capital expenses for a mobile mending business. Other funds have been given directly to other charities, including the Princes Trust, who then redistribute the funds to their user groups. The sole stipulation is that funds must go to people or organizations in the Rhondda area, however it is clear from the lack of requests that many former employees lack the confidence to make formal applications for funds, and this is confirmed by local Regeneration Services. There is no provision for assistance or support to complete an application from any of the statuary bodies or third sector organizations in the area, so it is unclear what will ultimately happen to the £1.5 million given to Treorchy.

Conclusions

Mobilizing Resistance (2012) underlined a temporary transformation of the Treorchy employees during the struggle to fend off factory closure, where the predominantly female workforce, described by Blyton and Jenkins (2012) as passive, became through union intervention an organized and assertive unit, who clearly differentiated themselves from other garment workers, not just in the area, but on a national basis. Garment workers in Rotherham were not as effective as the Treorchy workforce in attracting media attention when Burberry announced the closure of their plant with the loss of a further 540 jobs only one year later, however Blyton and Jenkins (2012) point to a lack of leadership amongst union officers who failed to properly galvanize the Rotherham employees and work collaboratively.

Mobilizing Resistance attributes the success of the Treorchy campaign to the memory of the miner's strike in the mid-1980s, and the long and bitter struggle experienced by the whole town. Many of the women involved in the Burberry campaign remembered this strike, and this helped to motivate them as they fully understood the consequences of another major manufacturing loss within the area, which gave them a nothing-to-lose attitude. For many of the women I spoke to, the struggle has had an overwhelming impact on their lives, however Blyton and Jenkins argue that the call-to-arms was an impermanent one and that 'these workers were not transformed into a group of radicalized, politicized activists, rather they were momentarily 'liberated from belief in the legitimacy of the status quo'.' (2012: 42) However, I have seen how the struggle has left an indelible mark, and though I agree it has not radicalized them, it has certainly been an agent of change. To précis Skeggs (1993) the situation the women found themselves in did not mean that because they challenged their powerlessness, that they automatically moved into positions of power, but rather that they refused to be powerless or positioned without power – a process that happened moment by moment and at a local level.

Through this chapter we learn that a key element of the Burberry campaign was that the workforce and the unions were able to create a temporary relationship between the producer, the commodity and the consumer. Consumers were able to link this to media coverage of public protests in London, New York and Madrid, where Burberry prioritized company value above ethical values and responsibilities towards their own workforce. It's likely that although Burberry held their production workforce in low esteem, through the protests in 2007 those same workers were revealed as capable of taking value away. In contrast, we learn that the global ramifications of the company's decision to move the bulk of its production to China were marginal, and Burberry sustained only temporary damage to brand equity.

Despite this success, the brand developed strategies to overcome any financial setbacks, including a new product launch of the £13,000 Warrior handbag. I question how, in a time of austerity, a company would market a bag so costly that only a few customers worldwide could afford it? And why, given the global economic meltdown at that time, would anyone want to be seen with this handbag? We can look to the merchandizing and marketing teams for some of the answers, as Burberry, not usually shy of using the trademark Nova check, used a different design, giving it a stealth value. Burberry, perhaps still fearful of international repercussions from the closures in Treorchy and Rotherham, nonetheless boldly went forth with a campaign championing Burberry's enduring Britishness, despite its slender use of UK production, with just a single plant in Castleford maintaining its connection to Britain. The Warrior handbag was promoted in a campaign featuring only British models, including model-of-the-moment Agyness Deyn, and members of British bands, who were photographed in London's Hyde Park. The campaign helped Burberry to fulfil its role as an authentically British brand, but it also captivated the imagination of consumers in international markets, who fell in love with a socially constructed image of England and its embodied qualities within the Burberry brand.

In the next and final chapter, I examine Burberry's attempts to manoeuvre itself away from press scrutiny over the closure of two important British production plants, and away from its links to working-class consumer culture, by showing how it inserted 'heritage' into its brand personality, using birth right and inheritance as a powerful tool in its economic development.

6

Heritage, craft and the global marketplace

Burberry's Autumn–Winter 2012 marketing campaign featured actor Gabriella Wilde and musician Roo Panes. Shot by Mario Testino in Greenwich, London at the former Royal Navel College, this image shows more visible elements of grandeur than the 2005 campaign featuring Kate Moss in a London mews discussed in Chapter 3. The clothing and accessories shown in this image include a fine wool and cashmere suiting; the studded gloves make a visual link to the early motorist's gauntlet, and the cast metal handle of the umbrella references a sense of craftsmanship and the handmade. Each element has been carefully chosen to echo Burberry's history as by 2012, and by its own admission, Burberry had become what Grieve (2013) describes as a media content company as much as a design brand. As the 2005 campaign constructed a hybrid image of Britishness and class culture, the 2012 promotion built an image of heritage Britain using these highly specific visual cues.

Embodying 'heritage' in-store

Burberry's 2012 campaign reflected changes in the British economy that emerged from political and economic shifts dating from the early 1980s. Moor describes a significant development from this era relating to a wider economic context set up by a Republican government in the United States and a Conservative government in the UK, which saw a decline in manufacturing and a growth in the service sector.

> The disappearance of the manufacturing industry from entire regions led to the reinvention of those areas through forms of service delivery; the growth of 'the heritage industry' was one area that provided much of the basis for the growth in events and exhibition design and for various kinds of architectural and retail design work. (Moor, 2007: 35)

Figure 6.1 Gabriella Wilde and Roo Panes for Burberry, Autumn–Winter 2012.
Photograph © Mario Testino. Image provided by Art Partner New York; all clothes and accessories by Burberry.

This shift away from making and the transition into service-led work required a fundamental rethink in some sectors of British industry, including the fashion and textiles industries. Back in 2000, under Rose Marie Bravo's control, Burberry's plans to launch a global network of stores were fairly advanced, and in that year the brand opened two important retail venues – a flagship store in London's New Bond Street and their first standalone store in Japan, in Tokyo's prestigious Ginza district. Both sites shared a long history of luxury shopping and they became significant elements of Burberry's new corporate identity that placed 'heritage' at its centre. The Bond Street and Ginza stores gave consumers, financiers, shareholders, competitors, the press, the general public and its own staff a clear sign that Burberry intended to re-establish links to the luxury fashion sector, and as Bravo 'pulled the brand out of small tourist shops' (*Economist*, 2001) the turnaround was astonishing, prompting the *Economist* (2001) to report that in the space of a year the label 'shunned by all but Asian tourists for its naff plaid-lined raincoats' had been reborn.

That the brand had its own long history added to the legitimacy of inserting heritage into its core values, and combining retail with heritage was a way that Burberry could communicate those values to global markets. Corner and Harvey examine the transference from manufacturing to service industry in some depth, concluding that merging 'enterprise' with 'heritage' helped to officially mobilize and manage change 'at the level of national culture and its attitudinal deep structure' (1991: 45). They agree that although both enterprise and heritage played an important political and ideological role before the 1980s, both terms underwent a radical reorganization during the decade and saw them emerge as specifically interconnected, and it was into this framework that Burberry emerged in the early twenty-first century.

Bloomsbury girl

One of the first clear manifestations of a liaison between heritage and retail at Burberry was the Autumn–Winter 2004 ready-to-wear collection, designed by Christopher Bailey. Bailey was appointed as Design Director in 2002, and his first series of collections were considered to be unremarkable renditions of the military-sport theme that Style.com claimed had 'surfaced on so many other runways' (Mower, 2002). However, in the Autumn–Winter 2004 collection, a sense of heritage was strongly evident, prompting *British Vogue* to report that 'this was a collection inspired by Virginia Woolf and the other "thinkers" of the interwar period' (*British Vogue*, 2004). Bailey explained that the collection was 'all very English [and] kind of reviewing the era's romanticism in a modern way' (2004). The image of Lily Donaldson as 'Virginia Woolf' makes an aesthetic link from Burberry to the Bloomsbury Group, an avant-garde collective of upper-middle-class artists and writers who formed an intellectual aristocracy that rejected bourgeois conventions of Edwardian life. We can see from the image that the trench coat is printed with a bold floral design onto a heavyweight fabric, and is reminiscent of the décor at Charleston House, the South Downs country home of Bloomsbury Group co-founders Vanessa Bell and Duncan Grant; the alligator handbag is fastened with a strap that resembles a horse's bit, which in turn alludes to both horse riding and hunting, outdoor pursuits that Buckley (2007) links to a classic element found in *Country Life* magazine, and which in the interwar years was still predominantly an aristocratic pastime. Donaldson's hair is styled to look like Woolf's own long, shingled hair, tied back, but not cut short and the unruly wisps of untied hair reflect Woolf's own messy hairdo, which was regarded as Bohemian in the early 1920s.

Much of the 2004 marketing campaign was shot in a space that resembled a stripped-back artists' studio, with lime-washed walls and dusty bare floorboards.

Figure 6.2 Lily Donaldson for Burberry, Autumn–Winter 2004.
Photograph © Mario Testino. Image provided by Art Partner New York; all clothes and accessories by Burberry.

The sets were carefully dressed with paint-spattered easels, ladders and wooden stools. Lengths of canvas, string and rope sat next to pots of fat brushes atop tall jardinières, and old cleaning rags were positioned next to jars of turpentine. One male model wore a striped knee-length duster coat, another a white shirt, dark tie and a knitted cardigan; actor and model Hugh Dancy wore a velvet dinner jacket, white shirt and dark cravat, and all the male models had shoulder-length hair. The women were styled in above-the-knee satin evening dresses, paired with strings of long pearls and elbow-length gloves; high-collared trench coats had large-scale brooches pinned at the throat. The overall campaign signified a life of the aesthete, and as a piece of fashion merchandizing it proved to be highly alluring to consumers, though as a slice of fashion history its accuracy was questionable.

The Bloomsbury Group lived an appealingly eccentric life, and could be considered as worthy of preservation, but their life as intellectual artists was also an aristocratic one, and though they chose an alternate path that embraced feminism, sexual and political freedom, it was nonetheless a privileged life. But this campaign shows an aspect of life that many people from that era would struggle to recognize, as the interwar years in Britain were constrained by a crippling economic uncertainty. Historian David Cannadine links that uncertainty very firmly to the heritage industry, and argues that postmodern 'heritage consciousness' is broadly related to economic downturn, running from the last quarter of the nineteenth century, between the end of the First World War and the beginning of the second, and in the lean years after 1974, 'each one known to contemporaries as "the great depression"' (1989: 98). Cannadine points out that each of these eras was characterized by the formation of national preservation groups, including the beginnings of the National Trust in the late nineteenth century, the Council for the Protection of Rural England during the interwar years, and preservationist campaigns around Mentmore, Calke Abbey and the raising of the Mary Rose, which all occurred in the early 1980s. Cannadine concludes that this

adds up to a recognisable and distinctive public mood, which has twice come and gone, and which is now firmly entrenched in Britain once again: withdrawn, nostalgic, and escapist, disenchanted with the contemporary scene, preferring conservation to development, the country to the town, and the past to the present. (1989: 99)

Burberry's international customers seemed to agree with Cannadine's observations, and at a time when some sectors of British retail, and specifically fashion retail were feeling the after-effects of the dot.com collapse in the early years of the twenty-first century, business was good in Burberry's global markets, particularly in the United States, Europe and Asia. Bravo revealed to *The Guardian* her thoughts on why Burberry was a successful export ' "there is an admiration [for Burberry] in Asia and America and even Spain", says Bravo. "They like the British lifestyle and what they think it stands for – whether it's reality or not" ' (Barton and Pratley, 2004). Christopher Bailey, alongside brand consultants Baron & Baron, delivered a vision of Bravo's 'British lifestyle', reworking aspects of England's past to a global market that seemed thirsty for a sense of tradition found in long-established luxury goods companies.

Burberry was able to spread the heritage narrative to a wider consumer base after expanding its outward-facing communication from just print and billboard campaigns to online initiatives. Despite Bravo's fears about online selling, telling *The Telegraph* back in 2000, 'the internet is susceptible to the grey market and counterfeiting' (Mills, 2000) nonetheless, the brand started to build its online presence and Burberry's first transactional site launched in the United States in 2004. The role of new technologies and increasing importance of a strong online presence in the retail economy was built under Angela Ahrendts's leadership, and though she understood that it was important to site stores in prestigious locations, she also realized that traditional bricks and mortar shops were no longer sufficient in a widening global market, and that the way ahead was to develop an online relationship with consumers. Ahrendts is widely credited as the driving force behind Burberry's digital strategy and how it could link to a more lucrative 'heritage' culture, as *The Observer* reports

> But her relentless focus on reviving Burberry's heritage to the 'millennial' digital generation – which includes selling trench coats with mink collars, alligator epaulettes or studded leather sleeves – has worked wonders. Annual sales have more than doubled since 2007 to £1.9bn, and the share price has doubled since she took over in 2006 to £13.70. (Neate, 2013)

Ahrendts significantly developed Burberry's digital strategy from the outset of her tenure, and though it seems naturalized in contemporary fashion retailing, in 2006 it was a radical departure for a luxury retailer. Many premium retailers argued that online transactions devalued the face-to-face in-store experience, as there was no opportunity to see and feel the fabrics, examine the fit, or benefit from the expertise of the sales assistants. Even in 2012, Prada, one of Burberry's primary competitors, told the *Harvard Business Review* that they would not sell high-end collections online because they were 'concerned about compromising our image by using a channel where second-hand cars and books are sold' (Cartner-Morley, 2012). Ahrendts went against the flow of luxury fashion retail, and not only developed a digital platform, but started to target younger consumers through online initiatives in order to develop a new demographic for the brand. CNN credits her ability to understand how and where younger customers absorb brand values: 'But there's also been her ability to tap into a new generation of digital consumers relying on social media for fashion trends, and increasingly buying online' (McKenzie, 2013). However, Burberry's journey to a successful online profile took some time and their first digital platform – Art of the Trench, didn't appear until 2009, but the path that took them to this point gave the company an opportunity to examine their historic credentials and delve into a potentially lucrative heritage market.

Real English heritage

One of the first collections under Ahrendts's tenure was Spring–Summer 2006, which was also the year that marked the 150th anniversary of the company. The anniversary gave Ahrendts and the brand the right kind of context in which to celebrate its own heritage, and the ready-to-wear collection was characterized by a look back in time. Style.com reported a specific temporal context and design brief, stating that the inspiration for the collection was the Duke and Duchess of Windsor, and their 'extended sojourn in Paris' (Mower, 2006) while others were more generic impressions of a rural England, including *British Vogue* who likened the collection to 'all the colours of a walk in the English countryside' (Morton, 2006). Ahrendts later revealed in an article she wrote for the *Harvard Business Review* that from the outset of her appointment at Burberry, she was worried that licensing (which was still out of control despite the efforts of Rose Marie Bravo) threatened to destroy the brand's unique strengths and that her approach was to 'centralize design and focus on innovating core heritage products.' (Ahrendts, 2013). This move essentially placed Bailey alongside Ahrendts, and the two of them worked to design and deliver this vision. Ahrendts also told *Fortune* magazine that in 2006, she'd examined Burberry's competitors and made the decision to 'look backward to identify enduring strengths' concluding that 'we're British. They're not. How do we exploit that heritage?' (Leahey, 2012).

Ahrendts's plan to centralize British heritage surfaced through the festivities of 150th anniversary, and gave the British fashion media an opportunity to celebrate the brand, and particularly its creative director. *British Vogue* reported

Figure 6.3 Gemma Ward for Burberry, Spring–Summer 2006.
Photograph © Mario Testino. Image provided by Art Partner New York; all clothes and accessories by Burberry.

that 'Christopher Bailey has developed this label while staying faithful to its heritage and very proper British beginnings. [The label captures the essence of the childhood rose-tinted view of England that you never want to lose]' (Morton, 2006). Style.com added 'that such a whippersnapper has been able to turn the frumpy old country lady's Burberry into a fashionable thing for the first time in its 150 years is in fact something of a cause for national pride in Britain' (Mower, 2006).

The Spring–Summer 2006 campaign featured formal eveningwear for men and brocade cocktail dresses for women. The women's wear was accessorized with belted sequinned cardigans, and a cloche-shaped beanie, which lent a pre-war glamour to the collection, however the garment highlighted in the British press was a trench coat with fox fur cuffs and collar that attracted only a minimal level of protest when it was shown at Milan Fashion Week, but which nonetheless alluded to fox-hunting. Bolton argues that 'few sports seem more English than fox-hunting' (2006: 107) which rendered the garment into English mythology, particularly in a European and North American context. However, the links to Edward and Mrs Simpson and their supposed Nazi sympathies, and the use of fox fur did nothing to harm brand value, and Burberry's Profit & Loss sheets showed an increase of £6 million in this financial year (Sawers, 2007).

Burberry successfully developed heritage as a capital-producing element of the brand, and carefully judged the correct balance of 'heritage' as nostalgia, but this took the form of what Appadurai describes as 'nostalgia without memory' (1996: 30). Burberry understood that it could sell a sense of nostalgia to its increasingly large global market and potentially utilize one of the effects of globalization, what Robins (1991) describes as an increased mobility across frontiers. Robins argues that this mobility made it ever more difficult to maintain coherent and well-bounded local cultures and places, and Goodrum concludes that 'in view of this mobility, globalization at the turn of the twenty-first century is often related to a reactionary emergence of local nostalgia' (2005: 37). Goodrum also argues that the instabilities connected to globalization has 'generated feelings of insecurity and vulnerability, and that the folksy look with its signposts to a bygone age, craft production and homespun charm is being actively employed to offset this apparent global rootlessness' (2005: 37). Did Burberry use this sense of rootlessness to reimagine a national space?

The following year spelled an end to Burberry's run of good judgement and for Autumn–Winter 2007 Burberry showed a collection titled The British Medieval Mood. A company press release explained that the campaign used only British models and musicians who were sited against a backdrop of 'iconic argyle and Prorsum horse motif wallpaper' (burberry.com, July 2007). This helped to suggest an Old English context, but one that was brought alive by the addition of hip young models and musicians.

The collection was inspired by the Burberry Prorsum Equestrian Knight on a Charger logo and featured what Mower (2007) referred to as 'armour, tunics and jousting regalia'. Yet, despite using model-of-the-moment Agyness Deyn for their runway shows and the accompanying marketing campaign, the collection didn't ignite consumer interest. More successful was the redesign of the Knight on a Charger logo, which was trademarked in 1909, but updated for the twenty-first century. The image resembled a brass rubbing, a hobby popularized in Victorian Britain, whose devotees made copies of monumental brasses celebrating the life of medieval European nobility from the thirteenth to the seventeenth centuries. Holistically, the logo neatly captured a sense of all that seems respectable about British history and heritage and hints at elements that are worthy of preservation. The logo embodied a strong sense of narrative – the noble knight, defender of nation, is the embodiment of a

Figure 6.4 Lily Donaldson, Keira Gormley and Agyness Deyn for Burberry, Autumn–Winter 2007.
Photograph © Mario Testino. Image provided by Art Partner New York; all clothes and accessories by Burberry.

latter-day hero, however its use in the Autumn–Winter 2007 collections was a way of describing what Bailey termed 'chivalry chic' (Ilari, 2007). Burberry again tried to capture a successful heritage aesthetic the following season, in Spring–Summer 2008, this time spreading their historic influences more widely: 'Our rich Burberry archives were the starting point for this collection, inspired by Burberry's historic role in aviation, Shackleton's Antarctic expeditions and the strict military tailored uniforms of the British Sandhurst Military Academy' (Kratzch, 2008). However, this collection also failed to excite consumers, despite an advertising campaign – The Beat Goes On, featuring what Hilary Alexander (2008) described as an 'A-list of gilded youth from catwalk superstars to emerging rock n roll aristocracy to snake-hipped musicians from edgy indie bands', all selected from BoomBox, a legendary club in London's Hoxton that closed on 1 January 2008. Perhaps The Beat Goes On proved to be too specialist for international consumers, and shares in the company took a hit, dropping 16 per cent by mid-January 2008 (Finch, 2008).

However later that year, Burberry regrouped and delivered their Spring–Summer 2009 ready-to-wear collection, realigning their Old English history through a perfectly judged marketing campaign that correctly assessed consumer need for something gentle and stable. The collection was presented at a time of enormous economic upheaval within the Western economy, and at the height of the credit crunch and sub-prime-loans scandal, consumers were looking for reassurance and dependability in the face of an increasingly globalized marketplace. Burberry, essentially an old company carefully groomed for the contemporary market, seemed to satisfy a yearning for some sort of stability. Goodrum argues that 'in fashion too, a similar trend is evident, with the quest for authenticity, realness and depth assuming crucial importance in a fragmentary, postmodern world of signs' (2005: 37). Had Burberry begun to appeal to an increasing conservatism within global markets, where their authenticity and undisputed Britishness felt real and provided a safe harbour in choppy financial waters.

Burberry's chic rural idyll

Bailey intended the Spring–Summer 2009 runway show to resemble a tableau of 'little gardening girls [wearing] every kind of outerwear – from their rain hats to their silk dresses' (Jones, 2008). The collection was intended to be 'soft, very romantic, something familiar but something new and reflecting our company

Figure 6.5 Lily Donaldson for Burberry Prorsum, Spring–Summer 2009.
Photograph © Mario Testino. Image provided by Art Partner New York; all clothes and accessories by Burberry.

heritage' (Jones, 2008) and featured unfinished hems and faux-handmade patchwork handbags. *British Vogue* congratulated Burberry for its elegant restraint, and praised the fact that nothing was 'too extravagantly polished in these times of economic strife' (Jones, 2008).

The photo shoot for the marketing campaign took place at Petersham Nurseries in Richmond-upon-Thames, which though lacking instant recognition, the venue is nonetheless full of what might be perceived as a romantic version of an English country garden. Designer Antonio Berardi, underlined this sense of gentle rustic beauty when he wrote about the collection in an editorial for *British Vogue* (June 2008) referring readers to Robert Browning's poem 'Home Thoughts from Abroad', which starts with a memorable line 'Oh to be in England, now that April's there', and he continues the rural theme with 'Think April showers, English gardens and birdsong and you begin to get the picture' (Berardi, 2008). The use of Browning's poem gives an important perspective to international consumers, as the poet talks about an idealized England seen from distant shores, and as Burberry were still showing at Milan Fashion Week at this point, this allowed them to increase the mythology surrounding the aesthetics of English culture that helped to develop feelings of nostalgia. The area surrounding Petersham Nursery was also important to the heritage narrative, as neighbouring Richmond Park is a National Nature Reserve, and forms part of English Heritage's national portfolio. The site has a long relationship with the British Monarchy as it was established by Charles I in the seventeenth century; it is one of London's Royal Parks, and still retains the King's deer park, which makes it a magnet for international and domestic visitors alike, and further deepens the brand's entanglement to what *British Vogue* describe as a 'chic rural idyll' (Barnett, 2008).

Combining the rural with the chic is a long-running and paradoxical motif at Burberry, and it is one the brand returned to with the Spring–Summer 2009 collection. The campaign included British model Lily Donaldson who was used to personify a hip version of 'rural chic', and despite the collection hitting all the right heritage notes, Burberry were still able to use specific trademarks including the instantly-recognizable Nova check seen on the hem of Donaldson's smock dress. The smock echoes garments produced by Burberry for farmers and agricultural workers in the nineteenth century, while the *broderie anglaise* shirt alludes to high levels of craft skill and artisanship (although the fabric is produced in volume) and is used here to evoke feelings of nostalgia for 'the past', and the romantic qualities of the handmade. Corner and Harvey argue that the skilled craftsman is often appropriated to serve a very particular role within heritage, where their imposed toil is displaced and 'naturalised as displays of resourcefulness and quiet fortitude' (1991: 53) and indeed the entire Spring–Summer 2009 campaign references the handmade and the home-grown.

The setting for the photo shoot fits into what Corner and Harvey detail as changes in UK visiting preferences from the mid-1980s, which switched from 'the hall' (1991: 52) and refocused on to the industrial and rural workplace. Both settings provide a familiar backdrop as we recognize the displays of work and labour – even if we have no knowledge of the industry – and the products that dress these sets give us visual clues. Wright notes 'the increasing importance of personal "clutter" and household implements' (1985: 52) to tell a story, so the nursery setting in the Spring–Summer 2009 campaign, styled with terracotta plant pots, truggs, potting benches and watering cans gives us a contained version of the rural, but one that is more expansive than a domestic garden, giving the image a feeling of richness and abundance. However, where the stately home housed collections of paintings, sculptures, rugs and china, carefully cleaned and maintained over centuries, the workspace was not afforded such care, so dressing an historic place of work took on what Corner and Harvey

(1991) describe as an exhibition aesthetic, which though an important element, was not always an accurate one.

Initial sales for the Spring–Summer 2009 collection were encouraging however, the Wall Street Journal reported that Burberry's profit margin had been hit again, and 'customer caution' (Rohwedder, 2008) was cited as the main factor behind the slump, forcing the brand to again regroup and consider how to move forward. As the worldwide economic crisis continued, Burberry chose a more conservative route forward, deciding that in times of crisis it was important to 'go back to the DNA and the roots of what Burberry's heritage is about' (Trend Hunter, 2009) a position agreed by fashion journalist Hilary Alexander, who wrote in *The Telegraph* 'in times of economic uncertainty, so the fashion legend goes, hemlines supposedly sink faster than share prices. But designers, it seems, also find a sense of security in fashion's great comfort zone – tradition' (Alexander, 2008). The classic trench coat is arguably Burberry's most traditional product, and it became the focus of their new collections. However, despite the underlying traditional aesthetic, which called for very little redesign, this marked a radical departure for the brand, as it was their first major attempt to build a new consumer demographic that was entirely online in a project they developed in collaboration with Facebook. However, as Burberry preferred what Arvidsson (2006) terms a pre-structured consumer involvement – where the brand guides the consumer in the desired direction, Art of the Trench, though ostensibly a social media platform and open-access online gallery, was simply an extension of their marketing programme. The design of the microsite seemed to provide an opportunity for consumers to upload their own images of Burberry trench coats, however in reality, the space was tightly controlled by the brand. Burberry's content guidelines are clear that very few images will be selected:

> Not all photographs submitted will be published on Art of the Trench. We will use our absolute discretion when selecting photographs for inclusion. Please do not email us asking why your photograph has not been selected. Only a very few photographs are likely to be selected. We hope you will not be disappointed if your photograph does not make it. (Terms and Conditions, Art of the Trench)

Burberry's approach to Art of the Trench was to commission high profile photographers to contribute to the pages, and the site resembled a street-style photography blog, an increasingly popular aesthetic dating from the mid-2000s. Scott Schuman, known internationally for his blog 'The Sartorialist', was invited to shoot the first set of photographs to appear on the site, and his images gave the site an 'attractive, high quality content' (Bunz, 2009) but equally they lent it a repetitiveness, as images shot in cities as diverse as London and Shanghai shared common aesthetics. Burberry was vocal about their partnership with Schuman, and their approach helped in two specific areas: firstly, to extend the brand in precisely the direction they required, and secondly, to create value using data from a highly engaged audience. Burberry also benefitted from its links to New York-based Shuman, as it allowed them to create a new space between The Sartorialist's own international following and the Burberry site. Posts onto The Sartorialists's pages demonstrate this crossover as they use Schuman's tacit recommendation of the brand to investigate the Burberry trench coats for themselves, as this post shows: 'Barbara (9 November 2009) 'The immortal trench coat!!!! I've checked the Burberry website and those pictures are simply amazing. As always:)' (thesartorialist.com).

However, when an anonymous post on his site asks 'were you looking for people wearing Burberry trenches or were you carrying some around with you?' (thesartorialist.com, 9 November 2009) they inadvertently reveal how some shots were fabricated specifically for the site. In his on-site biography, Schuman describes Burberry's initiative as their 'groundbreaking social media-cum-advertising "Art of the Trench" project' (The Sartorialist, 2009). Art of the Trench, far from being a community-building platform and fan-site, was simply an extension of the brand in an online marketplace, and there were numerous reports from people who were invited to get involved in the campaign, including Swedish born, New York-based model, stylist and blogger Carolina Engman, aka FashionSquad, who revealed that 'Burberry invited me to take part in their Art of the Trench project back in September and now I can finally share some of the pictures from the shoot' (FashionSquad, 2013). Similarly, Chicago socialite, fashion blogger and former model, Candid Candace, was invited to take part in the Art of the Trench photoshoot that coincided with the opening of the Chicago flagship store in 2012. Amy Creyer of chicagostreetstyle.com was assigned for the shoot, and Burberry's invitation made it clear that although the trench coat was the focus, it didn't necessarily need to be the model's own: 'the shots aim to capture the personality of the individual wearing the coat, therefore, if you have your own trench coat we would love to photograph you in this. If not, then we will provide trench coat options for you' (Candace, 2012).

According to Business Today, Burberry's intention was to capitalize on Facebook's '175 million users' (Grieve, 2013) and the brand started to allocate marketing and public relations spend in order to build a dedicated team. *Business*

Today also reported the success of the initiative, which not only attracted a high volume of traffic, but also resulted in higher sales.

> In the year following the launch of the Art of the Trench in November 2009, Burberry's Facebook fan base grew to more than one million, the largest fan count in the luxury sector at the time. E-commerce sales grew 50 per cent year-over-year, an increase partially attributed to higher web traffic from the Art of the Trench site and Facebook. The site had 7.5 million views from 150 countries in the first year. Conversion rates from the Art of the Trench click-throughs to the Burberry website were significantly higher than those from other sources. By all metrics, quantitative and qualitative, the campaign was a success. (Grieve, 2013)

Each strand of the campaign, including the collaboration with The Sartorialist, and the partnership with Facebook, gave a public face to what had been a largely unseen act of purchase, and a demographic described by Lash and Lury (2007) as imagined communities were made real for both Burberry and its consumers. Men's wear blogger Cloud 10 by LV was typical of the demographic Art of the Trench was trying to reach, and he neatly sums up the aspirational qualities of the campaign: 'My dream is to own the classic tan Burberry trench … I am slowly but surely working towards that goal' (thesartorialist.com, 12 November 2009). Cloud 10 by LV's blogspot tells us that at this time he was a young black student from Ottawa in Canada, and that he worked part time for the Mexx fashion chain. He regularly blogged about men's fashion and lifestyle and 'likes' GQ, Kanye West for APC and Jay-Z. That he also aspired to own a 'classic tan Burberry trench' is an outward sign of the success of the Art of the Trench campaign and its positioning alongside other, cooler digital initiatives, in what Cova (1997) describes as linking, where the value of the product is fed by an exchange value originated by the consumer. So as consumers elaborate the brand through loyalty, esteem indicators and 'good feelings', brand equity rises, helping Burberry to extract value created by consumers and turn it into profit. The online initiative was a lot less expensive to operate than a print campaign, and it allowed the brand access to valuable consumer information, however Burberry stopped short of fully engaging its followers. Independent brand strategy consultant Brian Phipps argued that the Art of the Trench site

> does not seem to encourage high levels of user interaction. (Burberry states that it wants customers to be 'involved', but the level of involvement seems constrained. As a fan, one's role is mostly to 'celebrate' Burberry. Only positive clicks ('I like it') are allowed). (Phipps, 2009)

Although Burberry had gone some way of investing in consumer involvement, Phipps's quote shows that the company's use of brand management as an active process was deeply one-sided.

'Some Aristo' goes into the information age

There was little consumer involvement in Burberry's runway shows at Milan Fashion Week, however the brand used them as a platform to tell stories about English history and company heritage, and following the Spring–Summer 2009 runway show, that played with elements of the rustic, came this men's wear collection for Autumn–Winter 2009, which referenced a more industrial side to British history. Though the T-shirt forms a contemporary element featuring a historical printed portrait and faux jacquard pattern on the hem, the overall silhouette of the collection gave an impression of the Victorian era at the height of its sober approach to men's clothing. But this was not an aristocratic aesthetic of top hat and frock coat, but one associated with the Victorian working classes, signified by a narrow-cut, rough herringbone tweed coat with patch pockets and epaulettes, flat cap and a plain black shoe. Though this look seems distant from the bucolic abundance of Petersham Nurseries, it shares a sense of deception that Mellor argues is common in restaging 'heritage' aesthetics where viewers and visitors use a point of reference in which exploited labour and economic hardship were off-set by a supposedly close-knit community and sense of neighbourliness 'one might perhaps call this "nostalgia", but to do so implies quite a strong notion of misrecognition; a judgement that those memories of a lost, urban working-class *Gemeinschaft* are not merely consolatory, but also counterfeit' (1991: 100). The Victorian era referenced in Burberry's Autumn–Winter 2009 ready-to-wear collection became part of another idealized past, this time connected to the working classes, where poverty, disease and crime were rendered invisible, and though this is not uncommon in the fashion industry, the timing of this particular collection was fateful as it coincided with the company's decision to pull out of another British-based production plant, putting over 500 workers into unemployment. The mood at Burberry was downbeat, and press reportage towards the brand was largely hostile: *The Times* report on the less flamboyant collection was typical of many:

> There was no complicated explanation from Christopher Bailey after Burberry's show. Clothes, he said, should simply be earnest, truthful and nostalgic. Well,

Figure 6.6 Look 36 Burberry Prorsum Men's Wear, Autumn–Winter 2009.
Image provided by ImaxTree, Milan; all clothes and accessories by Burberry.

after yesterday's announcement of 540 job losses at the 153 year old company and closure of its sewing facility in Rotherham, south Yorkshire, it wasn't exactly time to be bathing in experimental glory.

Sales increase of 12 per cent in the last quarter proved that despite the redundancies, Bailey still knows what he is doing; even if he wasn't quite sure who the man on many of his printed T-shirts actually was ('some aristo' was about as much information as we got). In short, this was a solid, unpretentious collection, mainly in grey. (Olins, 2009)

Despite the job losses and the on-going bite of the recession, sales at Burberry continued to rise, and they did so on the back of a repositioning exercise that placed a distinct but hybridized sense of heritage at the heart of the company, this time by utilizing the company's birth in the industrial age. The Autumn–Winter 2009 women's wear collection shared a similar aesthetic to the men's wear show, and was described by *British Vogue* as a modern take on 'old-fashioned romance' comprising pleated silk chiffon cinched at the waist, thick tights and laced boots, which gave it a 'Victoriana feel' (Jones, 2009). *Vogue* also noted that this collection was 'another clever turn in the archives [that took] modern nostalgia' (Jones, 2009) as its theme.

Burberry further developed and embraced a range of digital technologies to launch their Runway to Reality initiative for the Autumn–Winter 2010 collection. The first attempt was aimed solely at 'VIP clients [who] were invited to key flagship stores to watch the runway show live on commanding digital screens. Each was provided with an iPad that could be used to order product direct from the catwalk, for delivery in an unheard-of six weeks' (Doran, 2014). Runway to Reality started to use Burberry's outbound logistics – processing and delivering an order, as part of its marketing strategy, and turned it into another element of its value chain. By redefining this very traditional component of its business, Burberry was able to optimize and coordinate what Porter (2004) describes as linkages, which also meant that they were able to reduce costs through better procurement technologies. Burberry showed how it could manage those 'linkages', which Porter argues is a 'more complex organizational task than managing value activities … given the difficulty of recognising and managing linkages, the ability to do so often yields a sustainable source of competitive advantage' (2004: 50). Burberry had refined its transactional data systems examining consumer behaviour as part of Art of the Trench, so it was in a perfect position to pinpoint new opportunities for revenue at different points in the value chain by adding value to the consumer experience via Runway to

Reality, but also by being able to capture and extract profit for the brand through those same systems.

Ahrendts's drive to use new technologies to manage seemingly disparate brand channels put Burberry on a more confident path, however the design elements remained static, and the company didn't deviate from its pattern of using the archive as a central design element, as the Autumn–Winter 2010 campaign shows. It featured military-style tailoring and aviator jackets for men and women, and Bailey told Style.com 'I was thinking of uniforms and cadet girls—but it all started when I looked at an aviator jacket in the archive' (Mower, 2010). Ahrendts had a clear eye for what she considered to be a pure brand, and Bailey's designs (and those of the design team) kept that purity on track.

Ahrendts insistence on a pure brand meant that Burberry projected a consistent experience across all elements of its business in order to stand out from what the Annual Report (2010–11) described as a cluttered consumer arena, arguing that 'sharp definition communicates the point of difference and informs consumer choice, while also conveying authenticity and integrity, which are vitally important to a heritage brand such as Burberry' (Burberry Annual Report 2010–11: 12).

Figure 6.7 Burberry Prorsum at London Fashion Week, Autumn–Winter 2010.
Photograph by Ian Gavan. Image provided by Getty Images; all clothes and accessories by Burberry.

In line with Ahrendts desire to create a high degree of differentiation, in the last quarter of 2010–11, the group launched Burberry World, a website that aimed to provide 'a complete expression of the brand with full e-commerce capability' (Burberry Annual Report 2010–11: 12). Burberry World was what Ahrendts described as a million-square-foot store, and it offered consumers access to the some of the brand's most important features, including 'heritage and archival imagery, behind-the-scenes footage of key events, such as runway shows and photo shoots, philanthropic activity and comprehensive product views and information – the site contains the most complete product assortment available for purchase anywhere' (Burberry Annual Report 2010–11: 12), and where Burberry offered customers access to an exclusive network of photographers, stylists, models, products and stores that had a genuine pedigree of history, brand value continued to rise.

The site gave consumers a consistent experience across all of its collections, and the brand was able to move away from a local approach where consumers took potluck with customer service and product range. The site also appeared to offer a high level of consumer connectivity, and campaigns including Runway to Reality and Art of the Trench cannily judged how consumers might 'elaborate' the brand. This helped to build a strong relational network not only for fashion consumers, but also within the technology sector where Burberry won a range of awards for its online initiatives, including the Best use of Tech in the Digital Economy, the People's Choice Award at the FITC (Future, Innovation, Technology, Creativity) in the Advertisement (Web) category, and it was also FWA Winner – Burberry Digital Experience Autumn–Winter 2010.

By 2011, Burberry's Annual Report stated that they were using digital content as the primary vehicle to engage consumers and to communicate brand identity. The brand also made a commitment to expand the digital team in order to develop rich bodies of consumer-oriented content around any brand activity, which meant that still images from their main advertising campaigns were enhanced with video stories, traditional product shots became video clips, and local store openings became global events through live-streamed productions, via Burberry Retail Theatre. This included digital innovations 'such as virtual trunk shows, which allow runway show viewers to select items for immediate purchase, [and] further immerse consumers in the brand' (Burberry Annual Report, 2010–11). The company used single focus data points during Burberry Retail Theatre events and follow Berry's argument that 'for every explicit action of the user, there are probably 100+ implicit points for usage, whether that is a page visit, a scroll etc' (Berry, 2011: 152). This allowed the brand to speedily pinpoint consumer favourites, and manage their inventory and stock movements more accurately. But it also showed that centralizing the archive as the key design feature was the way forward, and by enveloping these key aspects of 'heritage' in an ambitious programme of technical innovation in some sense placed Burberry back to its origin in the nineteenth century, when its founder created what was then considered a new high-tech fabric. This helped to indicate that the twenty-first-century brand was effectively mirroring the success of the historic company and carrying on its legacy for innovation.

The Retail Theatre platforms helped Burberry to maintain a firm grip on its presentational media, using what Lash (2002) describes as an event-like communication, where fans of the brand came together for a short period of time in the same way as they would for a live runway show. Invitations to these shows created a form of what Turow (2006) describes as niche envy, as Burberry used instant data mining to classify consumers and made offers based on a perception of their worth and value to the brand. Burberry also made use of relational databases, partnering with non-competitor companies including Verizon and Apple, and even co-developing a custom-built Blackberry application specifically for its live-stream retail initiative. Media attention on Burberry heightened during this period, but the focus was largely on the digital interface between the brand and its consumers as it moved forward with what was essentially a major change in luxury retail custom and practice. Bailey told *The Telegraph* 'So it's a big deal. It's changing the whole system of buying, and the whole cycle of production. Basically you can buy every bag that goes down the runway and every coat and all the make-up as well' (Alexander, 2010). Burberry created a surround-sound-and-vision for the collection that corralled 'the clothes, the music, the energy and the atmosphere' (Seares, 2010) into an exclusive in-store digital experience, however the 'real-time' event wasn't a fixed point, and *The Telegraph* (Alexander, 2010) noted that all the livestream in-store content was centralized, edited, personalized and broadcast globally from the Burberry headquarters in London.

By September 2011, Burberry introduced the Tweet-walk, a collaboration with Twitter, where backstage images of the Spring–Summer collection were shown to its Twitter followers minutes before the live runway show. *The Telegraph's* Digital Media Editor reported that 'the digital show will enable those at home to see the clothes before fashion's elite' (Barnett, 2011). The Tweet-walk project 'created an enormous amount of traffic on Burberry's Twitter page, catapulting both #Burberry and #Christopher Bailey into the social media site's worldwide trending list' (Warburton, 2011). The Tweet-walk helped Burberry to break the brands' mentions-per-minute record, and the backstage images received more than 50,000 views within half an hour of the show. Burberry's Facebook fans were also treated to a live-stream of the show, and the brand created a link for 'every one of its eight million fans to stream the show through their own personal profile pages' (Barnett, 2011). The invitation to interact with the brand created a feeling of goodwill towards the company, as Facebook fans and Twitter followers were given an elite status, one that was comparable with VIP guests at the live runway show, however Turow (2006) argues that it also put pressure on consumers to provide additional personal details in order to achieve what he describes as better customer status.

Throughout the Twitter and Facebook initiatives, Burberry continued to deliver what *The Telegraph* described as 'detailed handcrafted pieces' (Barnett, 2011) employing what Armstrong (2011) termed 'textile craft techniques' and by 2012, this was partnered by the new, digitally enhanced flagship store on London's Regent Street – Burberry World Live. The store brought together the handcrafted and the digital – two seemingly disparate elements under one roof and acted as a denouement of Ahrendts's thinking and brand strategizing over the previous six years. The opening of the flagship store attracted national and international coverage from the architectural press, fashion media, financial news, social channels, brand experts and creative consultants. Burberry put together a downloadable PDF fact sheet on the building, titled 'Celebrating Heritage Through Best of British Design & Craftsmanship', containing a history of the Regency building, constructed in 1820. Extracts from the fact sheet showed how Burberry brought elements of British heritage together with in-store technology and digital innovation under one roof to seamlessly deliver a vision of their brand values.

> Made in Britain: In restoring Burberry Regent Street, Christopher Bailey worked in partnership with the best of British craftspeople including master carpenters, stonemasons, metal workers, welders, specialist gilders, decorative plasterers, cabinet makers, mill workers, wood carvers and joiners. [The store] houses British-made bespoke lanterns, furniture, plasterwork and floors. (Burberry Regent Street Fact Sheet, 2012)

It is clear that the restoration of the Regent Street flagship store wasn't a run-of-the-mill shop fit, but a physical manifestation of the brand, where technology was 'woven throughout the period architecture of the building' (Burberry Regent Street Fact Sheet, 2012) in order to give customers an immersive audio–visual experience within a heritage setting. A 6.9 metre screen (the tallest indoor retail screen in the world) dominates the main floor, showing films from some of

Figure 6.8 Betty Kirby-Green and Flying Officer Arthur Clouston with Burberry plane, 1937.
Image provided by Mary Evans Picture Library.

Burberry's best known sponsorship campaigns, including aviators Betty Kirby-Green and Flying Officer Arthur Clouston with a Burberry plane, who flew from Croydon to Cape Town in South Africa in 1937.

Mike Moriaty, a partner at retail consulting firm AT Kearney pointed out on CNBC news that 'Burberry has a long story, they are an Asia story and they have figured it out. The Asian consumer loves a very traditional story' (Shin, 2012) and so genuine historic links like the flight to Cape Town by Clouston and Kirby-Green help to immerse the Asian consumer further into the brand. However, Burberry.com and its counterpart, the flagship store on London's Regent Street, helped to convey a sense of the brands' tradition not only to the emerging Asian market, but to the global marketplace, and the 'long story' was just one of multiple approaches of deepening consumer engagement with the brand, as Bailey told the financial review site afr.com 'people arrive at Burberry.com from many different entry points', said Bailey, 'because that's how the internet works. They might find us through music, for example' (Cartner-Morley, 2012).

Ahrendts used the fact that '60% of the world's population is under 30' (Leahey, 2012) to determine that Burberry's long term aim was to attract the under 30 millennial consumer, and in an interview with *Fortune* magazine, she revealed that at the outset of her appointment at Burberry, she'd brought in research consultants who produced figures showing that in growing global markets this was also 'where the high net worth customers are' (Leahey, 2012) and that Burberry's future hinged on this market. By using new technology to present archive images and footage, alongside promotional films for musicians and singers signed to Burberry Acoustic (which were also available on YouTube and iTunes) Burberry signalled to its global consumer fan-base that as a luxury British brand with a strong sense of its own history, it was also a hip one. Many consumers had a purely online relationship with the brand, and Burberry's social media platforms Art of the Trench, Runway to Reality and Burberry Acoustic were used as a way of ensnaring this digitally savvy demographic, offering distinct entry points to ensure there was plenty to choose from. Burberry's social media feed reflected consumer fascination with the heritage elements of the brand, but also its strong ties to Britain, for example on Instagram

A 158-year-old company with a distinctly British attitude

From the mill to the workshop discover the craftsmanship of the Burberry heritage scarf

Google+

Crafting the Burberry heritage trench coat – from the iconic check lining to the hand stitched collar

Woven in Scotland – discover the unique craftsmanship of the Burberry heritage scarf

Pinterest

Made in England – rolling hills behind the Burberry mill in Keighley, where cotton gabardine is woven

The label of the Burberry heritage trench coat features the Burberry Knight motif – a winning entry from a design completion circa 1901

The text refers to the handmade and the bespoke, and underlines the specialist roles played by British crafts people. Revisiting Corner and Harvey's (1991) assertion that the skilled craftsman is often appropriated to serve a very particular role within heritage, we clearly see that Burberry's text is intended to emphasize an aspect of rare and valuable skilled artisanship. Ahrendts' aim of 'nabbing those digital natives' (Leahey, 2012) went to the heart of the organization, as she built an employee base that could communicate with a millennial audience through digital and social media: 'that's their mother tongue', she says of young people. Today, 70 per cent of Burberry employees are under 30, and 40 nationalities are represented in her London office alone'. (Leahey, 2012). Ahrendts business model closely follows Olins's (1978) call for a more total approach to corporate communications – one that is concerned with external and internal perceptions of the corporation, and one that can bring about behavioural change.

By the time the Autumn–Winter 2012 campaign was shot, the brand was following a clear aesthetic pattern, embodied in their choice of models, venues, photographer, clothes and accessories. The Burberry press office reported that this campaign was their largest production shoot to date, and was approached 'on a cinematic scale'. The press release stated that the brand had created a series of story-telling videos which aimed to give context to the clothing collection for the first time, and actor Gabriella Wilde and musician Roo Panes (who was signed to Burberry Acoustic) were assigned to front the promotion as a 'romantic couple'. Burberry commissioned a series of six short films – London Mist, The Encounter, Greenwich by Night, The Icons, London Streets and Midnight Rain, and each one-minute film was accompanied by a soundtrack written by Panes and released onto Burberry's YouTube, Facebook, Twitter, Instagram, Google+ and Pinterest pages, and was simultaneously available to buy on iTunes. A special gallery was created on the Burberry site that allowed customers to buy directly from the promotional films using a special app, and there was also a link to the Burberry Acoustic pages. The films helped Burberry to conjure a strong sense of 'old London', and the use of the models as a romantic couple helped to make a connection between the heritage brand and younger consumers. Posts by subscribers on Burberry's YouTube site described how the films made them feel about Panes and Wilde – 'nah i love this one better than cara and eddie, cause gabriella and roo version seems so mysterious and elegant and stunning and intense at the same time' (krn strong, August 2013), while other posts concentrate on Panes's ineffable qualities of 'looking hot' (Danielle Flakes, September 2012) and his ability to model and write songs ' "So the dude who's modeling is also singing the song. Wow, I'm so jealous." XD' (Peter Cho, October 2012) However, Alex Mora and Charlie Lefty sum up what Burberry must have hoped to achieve from their investment

> I don't know if I'm in love with the clothes or the people or the music or the british style or ... Oh! Wait! I'm in love with Burberry!! <3 :) (Alex Mora, YouTube: August 2012)
>
> ' "Good Music + British Style + Cool People = Burberry." ' (Charlie Lefty, YouTube: July 2012)

Burberry's end-of-year profits for 2011–12 reflected a rise of 24 per cent 'resulting from growth in every single product category and global region' (Milligan, 2012) and after the success of initiatives including the Tweet Walk from 2011–12, it is unsurprising that they invested so heavily in this campaign, where pre-tax profits for 2012–13 showed an increase of 14 per cent (Burberry Annual Report, 2012–13) demonstrating how well each element of this campaign had been judged by Burberry. *Marketing Magazine* concentrated on the digital and creative aspects of Burberry's Autumn–Winter 2012 campaign, and in an interview with Bailey he described how the campaign 'celebrates our brand and London through imagery, film, music, weather and our iconic outerwear in a very British way' (Clark, 2012). *Marketing Magazine* praised the interactivity of the campaign, reporting that Burberry had significantly boosted its digital profile by allowing consumers to buy from the collection 'ahead of traditional drop dates' (Clark, 2012). But the campaign was more than just a chance of receiving an early delivery, as Burberry had utilized what scientific data analysts WaveMetrix referred to as the 'people-talking-about-this' metric, and successfully converted hundreds and thousands of likes on its social networking pages into sales.

We can see from the YouTube comments how Burberry customers had stated to weave their own stories into the brand (e.g. by imagining the relationship between Panes and Wilde, and comparing them to the previous incumbents – actor Eddie Redmayne and model Cara Delevingne) encouraged by the images the company used in their outward-facing communications. The mix of British models, actors and musicians, combined with souvenir images of London that stood in for Britain, led WaveMetrix to report an increase in consumer association between Burberry and 'British heritage'. 'The London photographs spread Burberry's British heritage: 42% of comments on the London photographs associate Burberry with Britishness, saying it "embodies British style" for example' (Bulman, 2012). A strip of images from Burberry's Instagram pages in September 2012 showed how the company created a strong sense of narrative, history and inclusivity via its user interface.

> British model @CaraDelevingne at the #LiveAt121 event in the Burberry Regent Street store tonight (131,148 likes; 197 comments)
>
> The golden #Burberry balloons – sighted over Trafalgar Square #London this afternoon (21,492 likes; 155 comments)
>
> The #Burberry Blaze Bag in degradé duchess satin backstage at the S/S 2013 show #LFW (19,153 likes; 390 comments)
>
> The #Burberrygifts swoop over Tower Bridge as they continue their festive #London journey (23,255 likes, 193 comments)'

The text is concise and the sequence of the images was very specific, starting with a shot of Cara Delevingne, who receives the most likes. The Burberry social team made use of the hashtag to promote a party at the Regent Street store, where Delevingne, a globally recognized model, was making an appearance later that day, and this event drove site traffic upwards again as followers were eager to see her. Delevingne was positioned next to an image of Trafalgar Square, and the social team uses an ongoing but vague travelogue narrative of the Burberry gifts/balloons as a device to link the brand back to an historic and easily recognized London landmark. A close up of the 'degradé duchess satin' purse from the new collection is sandwiched between an image of Trafalgar Square and Tower Bridge, and this helps to cement the relationship between the apparently disparate elements of Burberry, heritage Britain, the twenty-year-old Delevingne and London Fashion Week. WaveMetrix reported that the photo posts contributed to an increase in traffic on Burberry's social media sites (where posts to Google+, Pinterest, Twitter and Facebook were almost identical) 'as they are posted almost every day and receive a high number of likes and comments' (Bulman, 2012). According to WaveMetrix, conversion from 'likes' into sales and revenue can be a major stumbling block for many luxury brands, however Burberry, who in September 2012 (when this Instagram sequence appeared) had an international fan base of over eight million across its social media platforms, had no trouble in encouraging their followers to engage with specific messages and follow through to make a purchase.

By 2013, Burberry deepened its links to the past through the use a nineteenth-century 'virtual' calling card on Facebook. A handwritten note invited followers to watch the live runway show, and appeared to be from Christopher Bailey himself. 'A handwritten note to Burberry Facebook fans from Christopher Bailey "Watch the show live on the Burberry Facebook page today, 4pm London time". *Nearly there … Hope you enjoy the show today! Christopher*' (18 February 2013). The calling card was historically used as a way of entering the elite social circle of the British aristocracy, but it also served as mechanism to keep out 'social aspirants who could be held at a distance until they could be properly screened' (Hoppe, 2014). Nonetheless, in 2013, Burberry used the calling card as a sign of etiquette, which helped to feed a notion of exclusivity (despite Burberry's massive Facebook following) and further emphasized the connection between heritage Britain and Burberry. Also in February 2013, an image of a brass nameplate, digitally personalized in response to followers who re-tweeted one of its images appeared on Burberry's Twitter site: the Piece of the Runway image captured Burberry's heritage aesthetic, whilst still appealing to premium fashion consumers, it acted as a reward for engaging with the content, helped to create a personal attachment with the brand, and it's also likely that recipients shared the images amongst their friends. The digitized 'brass' nameplate created by Burberry's social team alluded to the handmade and historic nature of engraving, and to long-term product identification that could survive the wear and tear of continued use. Concurrently, Burberry ran the Smart Personalization sales strategy where, for a limited time, VIP customers were able to have their name engraved into a real metal coat tag or bag plate. The Twitter Piece of the Runway drive ran alongside the Smart Personalization campaign, and may have been an attempt to attract younger consumers to not only connect with the brand, but to make a purchase. The digitized image was exciting for Twitter followers that were featured in the promotion, as it bestowed a preferred customer status, however the 'gift' from Burberry helps the brand to achieve what Mauss (1950) describes as making and remaking social relationships, which he argues have a relational purpose, making the recipient feel compelled to give something back as they feel bound to the brand.

The pace of Burberry's digital and in-store marketing took off towards the end of 2013, and their offline and online activities became increasingly integrated when the company's festive van was seen on the streets of London. The festive van first appeared in 2012 as one element of their Christmas marketing scheme, when its sole job was to circulate around its London stores and other iconic London locations, and updates on the van's journey were posted onto Burberry's social media platforms including Instagram and Twitter. But in 2013, the brand stepped up its campaign, and invited customers to participate in the Burberry with Love social networking campaign, which gave those who signed up free entry to a prize draw that saw the 'Burberry Festive Van turn up to the winners homes and deliver their selected product' (Identica Chronicles, 2013). The custom-built faux-vintage van was emblazoned with company livery and a specialist roof rack carrying gift-wrapped Burberry products. The goods on display were easily seen from the street, and these deliveries – which are fundamentally a routine outbound logistic, again become a form of marketing, as images of the van were circulated to millions of global fans via Burberry's social feed, showing instantly recognizable sites including St Paul's cathedral and Tower Bridge, sharing similar characteristics to the Delevingne Instagram strip from 2012. The images of the festive van summoned an ideal Christmas spent in London, and indeed the range of images used in the Burberry with Love campaign included a perfectly snow-covered Regent Street, rosy-cheeked children dressed in tiny Burberry trench coats carrying branded gift boxes festooned with ribbon, and an elegant couple battling against a turbulent wind shielding under a Burberry check umbrella, all of which offered the consumer something sociable and inviting, but also something deeply nostalgic and conservative

Conclusions

This chapter shows how Burberry learned how to add value to the brand by loading products and marketing materials with a symbolic sense of heritage, and though we see the company falter on occasion, they eventually found their way and stayed firmly to a winning formula where the 'archive' was centralized as a design direction and changes to the main collection were minimal.

Both CEOs – Rose Marie Bravo and Angela Ahrendts, used the term 'heritage' in distinct ways: Bravo used important geographical sites, including London's Bond Street and Tokyo's Ginza district, and mined their connections to a long and illustrious history of luxury retail to achieve a sense of heritage for the emerging brand. Ahrendts used heritage as a way of creating a 'pure' brand, and as a consequence of this desire, the wording 'Luxury British heritage brand Burberry' was used in every element of its outward-facing communication including press statements, annual reports and messages on its social feed, and we see how this tightly controlled use of words helps Burberry to prescribe its meaning in advance, while delivering the consistency that Ahrendts aimed for. The full effect of embodying heritage into its brand personality came under Ahrendts's leadership, starting in 2006 when Burberry began to rollout their digital communications, as this gave them the opportunity to access a huge global market in which they could develop this narrative. Ahrendts's decision to merge new technologies with aspects of Burberry's history and other more generic elements of England's past, accurately judged consumer need for reassurance and stability at a time when the global economy was shrinking.

This chapter shows how Ahrendts's business model closely resembled Wally Olins's (1978) description of the 'new trading communities' that were still in their formative stages during the late 1970s, and the retail landscape that Burberry looked out onto in the mid-2000s mirrored a similarly new era, as the company understood that many consumers, and particularly the under-thirties, enjoyed a primarily online relationship with the brand, and it became one of the few luxury brands that communicated with its consumers using digital initiatives and social media platforms. Burberry seemed conscious of the social networking platforms emerging in the mid-2000s, and under Ahrendts's guidance the brand was already looking at potential collaborations to further immerse the consumer in to the brand. And though Burberry's first online initiative – Art of the Trench, launched in 2009, it's important to note that this was still one year before the advent of Instagram.

This chapter highlights Burberry's role in harnessing new technology to capture market share, and that they are considered to be one of 'the world's most digitally competent luxury brands' (Seidler, 2013) however they are disinclined to fully engage with social media platforms or their followers. On Twitter (home of the Tweetwalk in 2011) for example, the brand does not respond to other Twitter users through their feed, as their tweets are essentially pre-planned marketing messages. Similarly on Pinterest, Moth (2013) argues that because 'every single pin was either uploaded by Burberry or links to its ecommerce store' it makes Burberry look as if it 'shies away from actively engaging with its followers', however Moth, in common with many brand consultants, argues that this adds to their allure 'as it remains aloof and exclusive rather than being friendly and accessible.' (Moth, 2013) Burberry used a plethora of in-house microsites including Art of the Trench, Runway to Reality and Burberry Acoustic as a way of enticing a wide range of consumers to the brand, providing what Henrion and Parkin describe as 'many points of contact with various groups of people' (1967: 7) but one that has been finessed into a single brand channel, and is able to withstand consumer scrutiny.

Though Burberry remain distant from its own workforce, they nonetheless fell back on an aesthetic that referred directly to the labour process, and some of the products to emerge under Ahrendts's tenure include the faux hand-stitched *broderie anglaise* fabrics and rustic smocks from the Spring–Summer 2009 collection, and the metal castings and traditional tweeds in the Autumn–Winter 2012 collection, all of which allude to the handmade, and effectively turn the products into signs of a classic and comforting heritage narrative. This chapter shows that Burberry actively combined labour with the design process to produce products that are, aesthetically at least, strongly connected with the skilled production of the past. The products are also indicative of handmade couture garments, helping to boost company revenue through this profitable connection as they correspondingly command a higher price in the global marketplace. Similarly, the new flagship store on London's Regent Street played an important role in underlining Burberry's links to the handmade, and where the 2009 and 2012 ready-to-wear collections capitalized on a craft aesthetic in the fabrics and cast metal buckles and handles, the authentic craftsmanship within the flagship store gave the brand ample opportunity to refer consumers to the value of heritage via the skilled artisan, which was embodied in the fine plasterwork, bespoke furniture and custom-made stone masonry, and these very specific qualities, and corresponding images, were replicated on their social networking sites.

Another key motivation for Burberry to strengthen its connections with England, and specifically with particular aspects of English history and company history, was to strengthen its appeal within a global market. WaveMetrix showed us that Burberry's international fans responded well to easily recognized London landmarks, and when seen in proximity to Burberry products, consumers connect the brand with 'Britishness' and felt it to be an embodiment of 'British style'. Retail consultant Moriaty (Shin, 2012) tells us that within the emerging and lucrative Asian market, consumers of luxury goods love a 'traditional' story, and Burberry has become an acknowledged expert at tying brand image to tradition. Though it can be such a slippery term, Burberry indicate tradition through a narrow selection of images that includes Tower Bridge, Trafalgar Square, the river Thames and Big Ben, monuments and spaces that have no connection to the company but which signify souvenir London and are recognized the world over. Heritage can be seen as a force for good, yet in many ways it is a battle over private property, and a way of covering up all manner of social, economic and cultural ills. Burberry has cleverly used gaps in company information to present an image of the brand that irons out many of the unpalatable elements of globalized production and retail, and successfully used 'the past' to stabilize its future.

Conclusions

One of the key themes to emerge over the course of this research is Burberry's resolute determination to retain its sense of Britishness, and we've seen how their sense of the term emanates from outside the nation state. Equally, Burberry is described by Alison Goodrum as an iconic British organization, one that has become a 'byword for "authentic" British style [that has] built up a portrait of the nation in which [it] is free to dictate and define who and what belongs there' (2005: 18). And certainly, we've seen how Burberry has attempted to define who belongs at the brand, initially by embracing aristocratic and military stateliness as an important selling point and later on as both patrician elegance, and as party-loving and cool.

The British class system has impacted Burberry in multiple instances, primarily within the early years of the twenty-first century where ethnicity, in terms of white Britishness, started to matter. Kate Moss and Stella Tennant each provided a different paradigm of Britishness, and are polar opposites socially and culturally. We see how in the United States, these aspects of the brand became an important selling point as they were used to summon a fun-loving characteristic and an aristocratic eccentricity. Conversely, we saw how in the UK, ethnicity through whiteness created a class-based contradiction, which at Burberry can be understood as both white working class and the white aristocrat. And while Lawler (2005) describes how the white working classes are seen as lacking in moral values, we've learned that this can also be applied to the socially elite Otis and Isaac Ferry, as their lawlessness can be seen as a contradiction of this moral stance.

Despite this class struggle, Burberry's branding campaigns proved to be important in terms of distilling key elements of Britishness through choice of model, venue and product in order to satisfy large and underpenetrated markets in China and the US, consumers that were identified by Rose Marie Bravo as being interested in the British lifestyle. And although Burberry depend on

Britishness as a key selling point, it has transcended mundane geographical links in order to conjure an image of the country through imaginative associations – the bountiful kitchen garden, rugged moorland and Regency architecture that help the brand to stay British without the need to produce its products in Britain.

The development of heritage products and brand channels helped Burberry to create links to a very particular sense of Britishness, one that Linda Colley describes as contradictory, characterized as it is as an 'asymmetrical, composite state full of different but inchoate allegiances' (1999). The distillation of both Bravo and Ahrendts's clear vision of Britishness contributes to Burberry's accounting of intangible values, and in its post-rebrand state, Burberry revealed itself as a master of valuing a multitude of British constituents.

Another cornerstone of the twenty-first-century brand was the centralization of heritage, and here the company rebrand in the mid-1990s was immensely valuable to Burberry, as it gave them an opportunity to create a hip version of heritage England for the export market. Both post-rebrand CEOs used an international eye to create a version of old England that delivered premium-price elements of tradition and expertise to consumers in a global marketplace. This shift also gave Burberry a chance to create a media content company that was used as a vehicle to tell stories about the company, and which eventually became a central element of Ahrendts's vision of a pure brand. The creation of an online identity and social media platforms that embraced heritage, alongside cutting-edge technologies helped the brand to significantly increase sales amongst a younger demographic, and their visible consumption of the brand, for example on Art of the Trench – an exclusively online platform – actively contributed to Burberry's meaning and value creation amongst this group. We saw how young consumers engaged with narratives of British history and tradition, which were carefully mixed with influential tastemakers and stars of Burberry Acoustic. The specially commissioned films provided a link between Burberry Acoustic and, for example, the site of the Autumn–Winter 2012 campaign at the Royal Navel College in Greenwich, but also at the Regent Street flagship store. Each backdrop gave strong visual cues to the brands' heritage and their history in another century, and we see how the images and clips work to create a connection between hip young British musicians playing live and the skill of the British craftsman, and both elements act as an interface to communicate key values about musicianship and craftsmanship. Although Burberry embraces the digital, they remain close to heritage as bricks and mortar, now exemplified in the refurbished flagship store on London's Regent Street (part of Nash's Regency Curve), which uses and self-promoted aspects of authentic craftsmanship – the stonemason, the wood carver etc. – through its online platforms, that narrate the building's rehabilitation to its former glory in 1820.

Burberry has successfully capitalized on what Robins (1991) describes as a powerful effect of globalization – that is, a growing mobility across national frontiers that makes it difficult to maintain coherent and well-bounded local cultures. Burberry carefully judged which elements of heritage London to include within the brand, and during the global economic crisis in the late 2000s, this manifested itself in a range of products and experiences including Art of the Trench, a mass-produced broderie anglaise fabric, cast metal umbrella handles and belt clasps, a return to the nineteenth-century farmers smock, and the Burberry gift van, a bespoke faux-vintage delivery vehicle seen on London streets at Christmas. We understand from Cannadine's (1989) research how economic downturn often proved to be a strong link to heritage consciousness, and Burberry has not only weathered some difficult financial storms, but has successfully navigated a passage that embraced carefully selected elements of the past alongside a range of exciting digital initiatives, successfully embedding a sense of stability for global customers both online and in store.

Aspects of contested labour and production also form an important element of this work, and in Burberry's case, media attention within the stoppages during the First World War and in the Treorchy closure effectively prised the lid off employees' work lives and exposed the inner production methods at Burberry, which in the 2007 anti-closure campaign included wage levels that had not previously been publicly revealed. We can see from consumer involvement in the Treorchy campaign that elements of production, including where products are made and by whom, became an important issue to luxury goods customers, but only on a temporary basis, as in this instance consumer boycott of Burberry was short-lived. However Moor (2007) offers a reason for this, arguing that this situation is largely as a result of a lack of political intervention, and not simply consumer apathy, and that ethical behaviour has been made into a matter of individual freedom, which neatly avoids confrontation between government and business. Equally, the large-scale structural inequalities between parent company and workforce combined to create an unequal powerbase, and it is hardly surprising that the Treorchy workforce felt overawed by Burberry's strength as a big business.

Burberry's departure from Treorchy marked a substantial loss of British fashion production capacity, and this was a major cause of concern for employees and their political representatives, but also to customers. In Burberry's case, where its produced clothing was both straightforward and problematic, as althoug it does not deliberately place its origin within the interface of the brand, nonetheless they successfully produced a sense of location through their branding campaigns. Burberry have made the most of its situated community, which now resides online, free and clear from its labour force. As the Treorchy workers became momentarily visible as a British-based workforce, they were replaced by unknown and UK-distant workers, who took on the production for Burberry, and were positioned within the market hierarchy as a marginalized group, unseen and unheard within the global market.

Despite experiencing two potentially damaging incidents exposing a hostile management style towards its production employees – one via a ruling government during the First World War, and a second through national and international media coverage of the Treorchy closure, Burberry continued to feature its labour force in their online marketing and within its network of stores, but as a form of idealized history. At its Regent Street flagship store in London, within its social media feed and throughout its e-commerce site, the company intertwined images of aproned men at cutting tables and looms alongside short films featuring cutters and tailors from the 1950s, which not only reinforced a gendered approach to production, but also underlined the brands' valuable heritage elements, an invaluable source of brand equity. The use of images of workers from a bygone era were made to stand in for its actual workforce, and they helped consumers to focus on elements of traditional expertise and craftsmanship within a contemporary retail context.

We see that from the outset of the company, Burberry used inventive methods to differentiate itself from other manufacturers and retailers of outdoor apparel, including celebrity endorsement and product placement on adventurous international expeditions. We see this inventiveness again over the course of the rebranding exercise in 1997, a rebrand that coincided with a rise in creative advertising in the 1980s and 1990s, which used lifestyle and motivational research as its basis. Here we see Burberry begin to differentiate itself from other companies in the same marketplace by developing a branded lifestyle in order to attract new consumers, initially focusing on Stella Tennant's chic rural life, successfully elaborating an existence of wealth and privilege, and we see Burberry reach out and communicate fluidly and confidently with younger consumers

A clear gender divide is evident in public reaction to working-class consumption of the brand, as within classic post-war subcultures attributed to men (including the Mods and the Zulu Warriors), who were thought to reject commodities or subvert their values, led to a development of subcultural *style*.

In comparison, women were thought to consume passively and to focus on fashion, and certainly in the online Review Centre bulletin board, there is an emphasis on the transitory nature of fashion, and its subsequent negative impact on quality. This lends male working-class culture the status of subversion, and wearing Burberry can be viewed as creative appropriation, and attempting to dress like an English country gent becomes a valued cultural practice. In contrast, we see that being respectable was important to working-class women, and in Britain's post-war era they used consumption for what Partington (1992) describes as a means of social betterment. However, the impact of Danniella Westbrook changed that perception, and she was used as an example of the drift away from the 'old' working-class values of thrift and respectability to the far-removed 'chav' culture, a gender-neutral epithet.

Middle-class consumption of Burberry can be understood as the construction of difference: where working-class consumption of Burberry was predominantly linked to the highly distinctive Nova check, and its wearers have been identified as sharing the 'same' largely retrogressive identity, middle-class consumers strive for difference and actively add value. We can see how Burberry caters to middle-class needs by offering a range of products and in-store and online experiences that develop an intimate profile of the consumer that simultaneously encourages difference and brand loyalty. This proved somewhat difficult during the moral panic surrounding working-class consumption of the brand, as luxury had visibly crossed class lines. However, we see Burberry challenge this position through the use of socially elite and titled women as models, following a pattern established in the 1950s and 1960s. Rose Marie Bravo hired Stella Tennant, daughter of the Hon Tessa Tennant and granddaughter of the Duke and Duchess of Devonshire; during Ahrendts's tenure the task fell to Gabriella Wilde, who is a descendant of the Anstruther-Gough-Calthorpe Baronetcy. Burberry's reimagined links to the elite Bloomsbury Group in its Autumn–Winter 2004 collections, and to the Duke and Duchess of Windsor for Spring–Summer 2006 deepened the brand's connection – real or not, to Britain's illustrious past.

Burberry's long life in fashion production and retail has seen it come through some of the biggest changes in British consumer culture, and their lifespan, stretching from the industrial revolution to the information age, reflects those radical changes, and the company underwent what could be described as a move from identity to difference, contradicting Horkheimer and Adorno's (1997) assumption that commodities, once made, circulate as identical objects, determined by the intentions of their producers. Burberry can be seen as an archetype of the construction of difference, and it has a history that moves from functionality, for example the trench coat as a garment to keep out the wind and rain, through to cultural product, via a trench coat worn by Kate Moss. I'd argue that Burberry, more than any other luxury fashion brand, spun out of the control of its makers for a few years in the mid-2000s and became highly contested in its difference, perhaps most famously in context to class hierarchy, but also its geographic location where the company trades on and profits by its Britishness yet retains only a small percentage of its production within the UK. The production of the brand's locality emerges through its marketing campaigns and its online and offline channels, which act as a medium within which ideas about design, class, heritage and labour are immersed and then reappear within its public interface. Ultimately, the Burberry brand has become emblematic of the diffusion of luxury fashion, evidencing the desire for, and arguably the democratization, of a luxury fashion brand.

Bibliography

Aaker, D. A. and Joachimsthaler, E. (2000), *Brand Leadership*, New York: Free Press.

Adamson, D. and Byrne, P. (2008), *The Treorchy Social Audit*, Pontypridd: University of Glamorgan.

Ahmed, S. (2004), 'Affective Economies', *Social Text 79*, 22 (2).

Ahmed, S. (2010), *The Promise of Happiness*, Durham: Duke University Press.

Ahrendts, A. (2013), 'Burberry's CEO on Turning an Ageing British Icon into a Global Luxury Brand', *Harvard Business Review*, January–February 2013. Available online: http://hbr.org/2013/01/burberrys-ceo-on-turning-an-aging-brit ish-icon-into-a-global-luxury-brand/ar/1 (accessed 6 May 2014).

Alexander, E. (2012a), 'Burberry's New Couple', *British Vogue Online*, 29 May 2012. Available online: http://www.vogue.co.uk/news/2012/05/28/burberry-casts-gabrie lla-wilde-and-roo-panes-in-new-campaign (accessed 8 October 2014).

Alexander, E. (2012b), 'Vogue News: Burberry Opens Regent Street Flagship', *British Vogue Online*, 13 September 2012. Available online: http://www.vogue.co.uk/ news/2012/09/13/burberry-regent-street-flagship-opens (accessed 8 January 2013).

Alexander, H. (2008), 'Burberry's New £13,000 Warrior Handbag', *Telegraph Online*, 8 January 2008. Available online: https://www.telegraph.co.uk/news/uknews/1574881/ Burberrys-new-13000-Warrior-handbag.html (accessed 5 March 2015).

Alexander, H. (2010), 'Burberry's Conquest of Cyber Space', *Telegraph Online*, 8 September 2010. Available online: http://fashion.telegraph.co.uk/columns/hilary-alexander/TMG7989381/Burberrys-conquest-of-cyber-space.html (accessed 13 March 2015).

Andy123 (2004), *ReviewCentre*, 3 September 2004. Available online: https://www.revie wcentre.com/review133671.html (accessed 4 August 2014).

Anonymous (2006), *ReviewCentre*, 7 August 2006. Available online: https://www.revie wcentre.com/review208859.html (accessed 11 July 2013).

Appadurai, A. (1996), *Modernity at Large: Cultural Dimensions of Globalisation*, Public Works Volume 1, Minneapolis: University of Minnesota Press.

Appadurai, A. (1986), *The Social Life of Things: Commodities in Cultural Perspective*, Cambridge: Cambridge University Press.

Armstrong, L. (2011), 'Tweet-Walk', *Fashionietzsche*, 20 September 2011. Available online: http://fashionietzsche.blogspot.co.uk (accessed 10 October 2014).

Arvidsson, A. (2009), *The Ethical Economy*, New York: Columbia University Press.

Arvidsson, A. (2006), *Brands: Meaning and Value in Media Culture*, London: Routledge.

Ash, J. and Wilson, E. (1992), *Chic Thrills: A Fashion Reader*, London: HarperCollins.

Back, L. and Gane, N. (2012), 'The Promise and Craft of Sociology Revisited: C Wright Mills 50 Years On', *Theory Culture and Society*, 29 (7–8): 399–421.

Baker, R. (2012), 'Burberry Launches Christmas Events', *Marketing Week*, 11 December 2012. Available online: http://www.marketingweek.co.uk/news/burberry-launches-christmas-events/4005090.article (accessed 11 October 2014).

Barnett, E. (2011), 'London Fashion Week: Twitter Teams Up with Burberry to Launch "Tweetwalk"', *The Telegraph*, 19 September 2011. Available online: http://www.telegraph.co.uk/technology/twitter/8773521/London-Fashion-Week-Twit ter-teams-up-with-Burberry-to-launch-Tweetwalk.html (accessed 3 October 2014).

Barnett, L. (2008), 'Burberry's English Lily', *Vogue.com*, 10 December 2008. Available online: http://www.vogue.co.uk/news/2008/12/10/lily-donaldson-for-burberry (accessed 28 August 2014).

Baron-Baron.com (2007). Available online: http://baron-baron.com (accessed 11 March 2022).

Barton, L. and Pratley, N. (2004), 'The Two Faces of Burberry', *The Guardian Online*, 15 April 2004. Available online: http://www.theguardian.com/lifeandstyle/2004/apr/15/ fashion.shopping (accessed 18 September 2014).

Baudrillard, J. (1968), *The System of Objects*, London: Verso.

BBC News (2004a), 'New Lines Lift Burberry Profits', *BBC News Online*, 24 May 2004. Available online: http://news.bbc.co.uk/1/hi/business/3741467.stm (accessed 16 September 2014).

BBC News (2004b), 'Pub Goers Face Burberry Ban', *BBC News Online*, 20 August 2004. Available online: http://news.bbc.co.uk/1/hi/england/leicestershire/3583900.stm (accessed 30 March 2014).

Bellafante, G. (2000), 'And Baby Makes Good Copy', *NYTimes.com*, 6 June 2000. Available online: http://www.nytimes.com/2000/06/06/style/front-row.html (accessed 11 December 2013).

Benford, R. and Snow, D. (2000), 'Framing Processes and Social Movements: An Overview and Assessment', *Annual Review of Sociology*: 611–39.

Berardi, A. (2008), 'Burberry Prorsum Crumpled Classics', *Vogue.com*, 22 June 2008. Available online: http://www.vogue.co.uk/fashion/spring-summer-2009/mens/burbe rry-prorsum (accessed 27 April 2013).

Berlant, L. (2000), *The Female Complaint*, Durham: Duke University Press.

Berry, M. (2011), *'Data Mining Techniques: For Marketing, Sales, and Customer Relationship Management*, Indianapolis: Wiley.

Bevir, M. (2005), *New Labour: A Critique*, London: Routledge.

Billig, M. (1995), *Banal Nationalism*, London: Sage.

Blyton, P. and Jenkins, J. (2012), 'Mobilizing Resistance: The Burberry Workers' Campaign against Factory Closure', *The Sociological Review*, 60 (1): 25–45.

Bok, L. (2004), *Little Book of Chavs: The Branded Guide to Britain's New Elite*, Bath, Avon: Crombie Jardine.

Bolton, A. (2006), *AngloMania: Tradition and Transgression in British Fashion*, New York: Metropolitan Museum of Art Publications.

Bothwell, C. (2005), 'Burberry versus The Chavs', *BBC The Money Programme*, 28 October 2005. Available online: http://news.bbc.co.uk/1/hi/business/4381140.stm (accessed 8 July 2014).

Bourdieu, P. (1986), *Distinction: A Social Critique of the Judgement of Taste*, London: Routledge.

Bowlby, R. (1993), *Shopping with Freud*, London: Routledge.

Bowlby, R. (2000), *Carried Away: The Invention of Modern Shopping*, London: Faber & Faber.

British Vogue (2003), 'Burberry Prorsum Autumn-Winter Ready to Wear' (12 November 2003).

Buckley, C. (2007), *Designing Modern Britain*, London: Reaktion Books.

Bulman, L. (2012), 'Burberry Use Social to Reinforce Their British Heritage Among Fans', *WaveMetrix*, 18 October 2012. Available online: http://marketing.wavemetrix.com/1210%20_WaveMetrix%20_analysing%20_customer%20service.pdf (accessed 15 August 2013).

Bunz, M. (2009), 'Burberry Checks Out Crowdsourcing with The Art of the Trench', *The Guardian Online*, 9 November 2009. Available online: http://www.theguardian.com/media/pda/2009/nov/09/burberry-art-of-the-trench (accessed 4 September 2014).

Burberry Annual Report (2007–8). Available online: http://www.burberryplc.com/documents/results/2008/17-06-08_annual_report/burberry_2007-08_annualreport.pdf (accessed 8 November 2012).

Burberry Annual Report (2012–13): 9. Available online: https://www.burberryplc.com/content/dam/burberry/corporate/Investors/ResultsReports/2013/6annualreview201213interactivePDFenglish/Reportburberryareview2.pdf (accessed 11 March 2022).

Burberry Annual Review (2009–10). Available online: http://annualreview2009-10.burberry.com/pdf/corporate_responsibility.pdf (accessed 25 September 2014).

Burberry Annual Review (2010–11), *Chief Executive Officer's Letter*: 12–15.

'Burberry Ltd.' (2018), *Encyclopedia.com*. 8 June 2018. Available online: https://www.encyclopedia.com/social-sciences-and-law/economics-business-and-labor/businesses-and-occu pations/burberry (accessed 29 October 2014).

Burberry Press Office (2014), 'Inspired by London, Burberry Flagship Opens in Shanghai', 14 April 2014. Available online: http://www.burberryplc.com/media_centre/press_releases/2014/burberry-flagship-opens-in-shanghai (accessed 15 August 2014).

Burberry Regent Street Fact Sheet (2012), *Emtecnica,* September 2012. Available online: http://www.emtecnica.com/burberry-regent-street-fact-sheet.pdf (accessed 17 October 2013).

Burton, A (2006), *Archive Stories: Facts, Fictions and the Writing of History*, Durham: Duke University Press.

Buttolph, A. (2008), 'The Making of Moss', *The Daily Mail Online*, 22 September 2008. Available online: http://www.dailymail.co.uk/femail/article-1059073/The-making-Moss-Inside-World-8217-s-Most-Famous-Wardrobe.html (accessed 19 February 2014).

Cable, J. (2007), 'Is That a Fake in Your Pocket? Quite Possibly …', *Reuters*, 23 July 2007. Available online: http://www.reuters.com/article/2007/07/23/us-fakegoods-study-idUSL2053515520070723 (accessed 18 July 2014).

Cadwalladr, C. (2007), 'Squaring Up to Burberry', *Observer Magazine*, 25 March 2007: 36–43.

Cadwalladr, C. (2012), 'The Hypocrisy of Burberry's "Made in Britain" Appeal', *Observer Online*, 16 July 2012. Available online: http://www.theguardian.com/commentisfree/2012/jul/16/burberry-china-british-carole-cadwalladr (accessed 11 December 2014).

Candace, C. (2012), 'Inside Burberry Chicago's "Art of the Trench" Campaign', *Chicago Now Online*, 28 November 2012. Available online: http://www.chicagonow.com/candid-candace/2012/11/inside-burberry-chicagos-art-of-the-trench-campaign/ (accessed 4 September 2014).

Cannadine, D. (1989), *The Pleasures of the Past*, New York: Norton.

Carlisle, L. (2008), *ReviewCentre*, 21 February 2008. Available online: https://www.reviewcentre.com/review327012.html.

Carpenter, J. (2011), 'Burberry: From Chavvy to Royalty as Kate Middleton Wears It in Belfast', *The Express Online*, 10 March 2011. Available online: http://www.express.co.uk/life-style/style/233760/Burberry-From-chavvy-to-royalty-as-Kate-Middleton-wears-it-in-Belfast (accessed 17 July 2014).

Cartner-Morley, J. (2012), 'Burberry Designs Store to Resemble Website', *Financial Review Online*, 13 September 2012. Available online: http://www.afr.com/p/technology/burberry_designs_store_to_resemble_uc9Q162awz1HNHPHMGlErO (accessed 26 September 2014).

Castell, M. (1996), *The Rise of the Network Society*, Cambridge, MA: Blackwell.

Chamberlin, E. H. (1933), *The Theory of Monopolistic Competition*, Cambridge, MA: Harvard University Press.

Chesters, L. (2012), 'Far East Fakes: The Burgeoning Underworld of Counterfeit Goods', *The Independent Online*, 9 November 2012. Available online: http://www.independent.co.uk/news/business/analysis-and-features/far-east-fakes-the-burgeoning-underworldof-counterfeit-goods-8301450.html (accessed 15 August 2014).

Chiesa, A. and Porch, L. (12 November 2003), 'Burberry Shown the Door as Bars Ban the Thugs' Uniform', *The Scottish Herald*. Available online: https:// //www.heraldscotland.com/news/12526061.burberry-shown-the-door-as-bars-ban-the-thugs-uniform/ (accessed 4 December 2013).

Chowney, V. (2011), 'Burberry Attempts "Mass Customisation" with Burberry Bespoke', *EConsultancy*, 4 November 2011. Available online: https://econsultancy.com/burbe rry-attempts-mass-customisation-with-burberry-bespoke/ (accessed 22 April 2015).

Clark, N. (2012), 'Burberry Boosts Digital Approach with Interactive Campaign', *Marketing Magazine Online*, 29 May 2012. Available online: http://www.marketingm agazine.co.uk/article/1134144/burberry-boosts-digital-approach-interactive-campa ign (accessed 6 Ocotber 2014).

Cochoy, F. (1998), 'Another Discipline for the Market Economy: Marketing as Performative Knowledge and Know-How for Capitalism', in M. Callon (ed.), *The Laws of the Markets*', Oxford: Blackwell, 194–221.

Colley, L. (1999), 'Britishness in the 21st Century', 8 December 1999. Available online: https://www.centreforcitizenship.org/docs/britishness.pdf (accessed 8 March 2022).

The Constant Gardener (2005), Film. Available online: https://www.imdb.com/title/ tt0387131/ (accessed 11 March 2022).

Coombes, R. (1998), *The Cultural Life of Intellectual Properties: Authorship, Appropriation and the Law*, Durham: Duke University Press; cited in Lury 2004.

Coopey, R., O'Connell, S. and Porter, D. (2005), *Mail Order Retailing in Britain: A Business and Social History*, Oxford: Oxford University Press.

Corner, J. and Harvey, S. (1991), *Enterprise and Heritage: Crosscurrents of National Culture*, London: Routledge.

Cova, B. (1997), 'Community and Consumption: Towards a Definition of the "Linking Value" of Products and Services', *European Journal of Marketing*, 31 (3–4): 297–316.

Crafts Council Spark Plug Curators Award. Available online: http://www.craftscouncil. org.uk/professional-development/for-curators/spark-plug-curator-awards/view/sin-weston/project (accessed 12 April 2013).

Craik, J. (1993), *The Face of Fashion*, London: Routledge.

Crane, D. (2000), *Fashion and Its Social Agendas: Class, Gender, and Identity in Clothing*, Chicago: University of Chicago Press.

Davies, A. (2009), *The Gangs of Manchester: The Story of The Scuttlers, Britain's First Youth Cult*, Wrea Green: Milo Books.

Deans, J. and Plunkett, J. (2014), 'East Enders Bosses Promise to Bring Spirit of Shoreditch to Show', *Guardian Media*, 28 January 2014. Available online: https:// www.theguardian.com/tv-and-radio/2014/jan/28/eastenders-revamp-gentrif ied-east-london (accessed 4 August 2014).

Dodd, V. (2005), 'Chanel and Burberry Drop Moss as Police Start Inquiry', *The Guardian*, 22 September 2005. Available online: http://www.theguardian.com/ uk/2005/sep/22/drugsandalcohol.vikramdodd (accessed 17 April 2014).

Doran, H. V. (1940), *Industrial Design: A Practical Guide*, New York: McGraw Hill.

Doran, S. (2014), 'How Burberry Does Digital', *The Luxury Society*, 10 January 2014. Available online: https://www.luxurysociety.com/en/articles/2014/01/how-burbe rry-does-digital/ (accessed 24 September 2014).

Drum, The (2003), 'Burberry Stained by Undesirable Clientele', 27 November 2003. Available online: http://www.thedrum.com/news/2003/11/27/burberry-stained-undesirable-clientele (accessed 3 July 2014).

Economist Editorial (2001), 'Face Value: Stretching the Plaid', 1 February 2001. Available online: http://www.economist.com/node/491000 (accessed 20 June 2014).

Economist Online (2011), 'Burberry and Globalisation: A Chequered Story', 20 January 2011. Available online: https://www.economist.com/britain/2011/01/20/a-checke red-story (accessed 3 March 2013).

Edwards, T. (2011), 'The Clothes Maketh the Man: Masculinity, the Suit and Men's Fashion', in T. Edwards, *Fashion in Focus: Concepts, Practices and Politics*, London: Routledge.

Fashion Squad (2013), 'Art of the Trench', 12 November 2013. Available online: http://www.fashionsquad.com/art-of-the-trench/ (accessed 5 September 2014).

Finch, J. (2000), 'Burberry's £2b Return', *The Guardian*, 1 December 2000. Available online: https://www.theguardian.com/business/2000/dec/01/6 (accessed 22 March 2022).

Finch, J. (2003), 'Burberry's Image Goes From Toff to Tough', *The Guardian*, 25 November 2003. Available online: https://www.theguardian.com/business/2003. nov/25/3 (accessed 4 August 2014).

Finch, J. (2008), 'Poor Sales Hit Burberry Shares', *The Guardian*, 16 January 2008. Available online: http://www.theguardian.com/business/2008/jan/16/retail.fashion (accessed 10 October 2013).

FootballForums.net (2004), 'Burberry Ban', August 2004. Available online: http://www.footballforums.net/forums/showthread.php/70805-Burberry-Ban (accessed 2 July 2014).

Foucault, M. (1977), *Discipline and Punish: The Birth of the Prison*, London: Penguin.

Fox, C. (2014), 'The Great British Model', *British Vogue*, May 2014: 188–95.

FWA, The (2011), 'FWA Winner: Burberry Digital Experience AW2010', 7 January 2011. Available online: http://www.thefwa.com/site/burberry-digital-experie nce-aw2010?category_id=2807 (accessed 29 September 2014).

Gabriel, L. (1995), 'The Unmanaged Organisation: Stories, Fantasies and Subjectivity', *Organisation Studies*, 16 (3): 477–99, in C. Lury (2004), *Brands: The Logos of the Global Economy*, London: Routledge.

Gamson, W. A. and Myer, D. S. (1995), 'Framing Political Opportunity', in D. McAdam, J. D. McCarthy and M. N. Zald (eds), *Comparative Perspectives on Social Movements; Political Opportunities, Mobilizing Structures, and Cultural Framings*, London: UCL Press.

Goffman, E. (1974), *Frame Analysis: An Essay on the Organization of Experience*, New York: Harper.

Gold, T. (2008), 'Infamy? They've Got It', *The Guardian*, 17 April 2008. Available online: http://www.theguardian.com/commentisfree/2008/apr/17/gender.filmnews (accessed 5 February 2014).

Goodrum, A. (2005), *The National Fabric: Fashion, Britishness, Globalisation*, Oxford: Berg.

Goodwin, B. (1989), 'Fashion: Bravo, the Pacesetter of High-Profile Society', *Los Angeles Times*, 22 September 1989. Available online: http://articles.latimes.com/1989-09-22/news/vw-767_1_high-profiles (accessed 27 February 2014).

Grieve, J. (2013), 'Entrenched in the Digital World', *Business Today Online*, 3 February 2013. Available online: http://businesstoday.intoday.in/story/burberry-social-media-initiative/1/191422.html (accessed 30 April 2014).

Hall, J. (2004), 'Burberry Brand Tarnished by "Chavs"', *The Telegraph*, 28 November 2004. Available online: http://www.telegraph.co.uk/finance/2900572/Burbe rry-brand-tarnished-by-chavs.html (accessed 7 August 2014).

Hall, J. (2011), 'Burberry Lays on the Mother of All Parties', *The Telegraph Online*, 13 April 2011. Available online: http://www.telegraph.co.uk/finance/newsbysector/retail andconsumer/8448841/Burberry-lays-on-mother-of-all-parties-to-launch-flagship-Beijing-store.html (accessed 15 January 2013).

Hall, S. and Jefferson, T. (1975), *Resistance through Rituals: Youth Subcultures in Post-War Britain*, London: Routledge.

Hampshire Cultural Trust. Available online: https://collections.hampshireculture.org.uk/topic/burberry (accessed 2 September 2021).

Hansard Commons Sitting (1916), 'Messrs. Burberry Oral Answers to Questions', 31 May 1916. Available online: http://hansard.millbanksystems.com/commons/1916/may/31/messrs-burberry#S5CV0082P0_19160531_HOC_299 (accessed 11 June 2014).

Hansard Commons Sitting (1917), ' "Government Contracts (Messrs. Burberry)" Oral and Written Answers to Questions', 15 February and 5, 6, 7 March 1917. Available online: http://hansard.millbanksystems.com/search/burberry+1917 (accessed 11 June 2014).

Harvey, D. (1990), *The Condition of Post Modernity: An Enquiry into the Origins of Cultural Change*, Oxford: Blackwell.

Hayward, K. and Yar, M. (2006), 'The "Chav" Phenomenon: Consumption, Media, and the Construction of a New Underclass', *Crime, Media, Culture*, 2 (1): 9–28.

Hebdige, D. (1975), 'The Meaning of Mod', in Hall and Jefferson (eds), *Resistance Through Rituals: Youth Subcultures in Post-War Britain*, London: Routledge.

Hebidge and Willis (1982), cited in Lury, C. (1996), *Consumer Culture*, Cambridge: Polity.

Heller, R. (2000a), 'Rose Marie's Baby Grows Up', *Forbes.com*, 27 November 2000. Available online: http://www.forbes.com/global/2000/1127/0324129a.html (accessed 4 December 2013).

Heller, R. (2000b), 'Can This Woman Do a Gucci on Burberry?', *Forbes.com/global*, 24 January 2000. Available online: http://www.forbes.com/global/2000/0124/0302050a.html (accessed 6 December 2013).

Henrion, F. H. K. and Parkin, A. (1967), *Design Co-ordination and Corporate Image*, London: Studio Vista.

Herman-Cohen, V. (2000), 'Burberry Faces Forward', *Los Angeles Times*, 5 October 2000. Available online: http://articles.latimes.com/2000/oct/05/news/cl-31474 (accessed 30 January 2013).

Herman-Cohen, V. (2001), 'A Champion of Planetary Plaid Power', *Los Angeles Times*, 25 May 2001. Available online: https://www.latimes.com/archives/la-xpm-2001-may-25-cl-2233-story.html (accessed 11 March 2022).

Hochschild, A. (1983), *The Managed Heart: Commercialization of Human Feeling*, Berkeley, *University of California Press*, in C. Lury (2004), *Brands: The Logos of the Global Economy*, London: Routledge.

Hoppe, M. (2014), 'Calling Cards and the Etiquette of Paying Calls', *Literary-Liaisons.com*. Available online: http://www.literary-liaisons.com/article026.html (accessed 8 October 2014).

Horkheimer, M. and Adorno, T. (1997), *Dialectics of Enlightenment*, London: Verso.

Huggins, J. (2013), '10 Surprising Things You Didn't Know about Croydon', *New Era Internet*, 5 April 2013. Available online: http://www.newerainternet.com/blog/10-surprising-things-you-didnt-know-about-croydon/ (accessed 29 January 2014).

'Hugh Dancy as Daniel Deronda' (2002), Television Mini-Series. Available online: https://www.imdb.com/title/tt0321897/ (accessed 11 March 2022).

'Hugh Dancy as Galahad in King Arthur Film Production' (2004), *IMDB*. Available online: https://www.imdb.com/title/tt0349683/ (accessed 11 March 2022).

'Hugh Dancy as the Earl of Essex in Elizabeth I' (2005), *Television Mini-Series*. Available online: https://www.imdb.com/title/tt0465326/characters/nm0199215 (accessed 11 March 2022).

Identica Chronicles (2013), 'Burberry Festive Van', 9 December 2013. Available online: http://www.identica.co.uk/ic/burberry-festive-van/#sthash.jxTkOIz4.dpbs (accessed 10 October 2014).

Ilari, A. (2007), 'Gloved Ones: The Handiest of Accessories Is in Fall's Spotlight', *Women's Wear Daily Online*, September 2007. Available online: http://www.wmagazine.com/fashion/accessories/2007/09/accessories_gloves/ (accessed 27 August 2014).

Imagine (2013), 'Rod Stewart: Can't Stop Me Now', *BBC Television*, 9 July 2013. Available online: http://www.bbc.co.uk/programmes/b036yl2v (accessed 12 June 2014).

IPKat, The (2004), 'Walpole Mobilises against "Made in the EU"', 20 January 2004. Available online: http://ipkitten.blogspot.co.uk/2004/01/walpole-mobilises-against-made-in-eu.html (accessed 14 May 2014).

Jameson, F. (1991), *Postmodernism, or, the Cultural Logic of Late Capitalism*, London: Verso.

Jansen-Verbeke, M. (1990), 'Leisure and Shopping: Tourism Product Mix', in G. J. Ashworth and B. Goodall (eds), *Marketing Tourism Places*, London: Routledge.

Jones, D. (2008), 'Burberry Prorsum', *Vogue.com*, 22 September 2008. Available online: http://www.vogue.co.uk/fashion/spring-summer-2009/ready-to-wear/burberry-prorsum (accessed 28 August 2014).

Jones, D. (2009), 'Burberry Prorsum Ready-to-Wear', *British Vogue*, 27 February 2009. Available online: http://www.vogue.co.uk/fashion/autumn-winter-2009/ready-to-wear/burberry-prorsum (accessed 9 September 2014).

Jones, L. (2008), 'The Luxury Brand with a Chequered Past, Burberry's Shaken Off Its Chav Image to Become the Fashionistas Favourite Once More', *Daily Mail*, 2 June 2008. Available online: http://www.dailymail.co.uk/femail/article-1023460/Burberrys-shaken-chav-image-fashionistas-favourite-more.html (accessed 2 July 2014).

Jones, O. (2011), *Chavs: The Demonization of the Working Class*, New York: Verso.

Kellner, D. (1993), 'Critical Theory Today: Revisiting the Classics', *Theory, Culture and Society*, London: Sage, 10: 43–60.

Kerr, C. and Siegel, A. (1954) 'The Inter-industry Propensity to Strike – An International Comparison', in A. Kornhauser, R. Dubin and A. M. Ross (eds), *Industrial Conflict*, New York: McGraw Hill, 189–212.

Kleinman, M. (2002), 'GUS Catalogues to Get "Youth" Overhaul', *Marketing Magazine*, 21 March 2002. Available online: http://www.marketingmagazine.co.uk/article/140334/gus-catalogues-youth-overhaul (accessed 18 June 2014).

Kollewe, J. (2012), 'Burberry Warning on Profits Wipes £1bn Off Stock Market Value', *Guardian Online*, 11 September 2012. Available online: http://www.theguardian.com/business/2012/sep/11/burberry-warns-profits-sales-luxury-fashion (accessed 13 October 2012).

Kratzch, H. (2008), 'Burberry Launches Prorsum Women's and Menswear for Autumn–Winter 2007–08', CoolestFashion, 4 January 2008. Available online: *coolestfashionof2009.blogspot.com* (accessed 10 October 2013).

Landesman, C. (2009), *Starstruck: Fame, Failure, My Family and Me*, London: Pan.

Lash, S. (2002), *Critique of Information*, London: Sage.

Lash, S. and Lury, C. (2007), *Global Culture Industry*, Cambridge, MA: Polity Press.

Lash, S. and Urry, J. (1994), *Economies of Sign and Space*, London: Sage.

Lawler, S. (2005), 'Disgusted Subjects: The Making of Middle-Class Identities', *The Sociological Review*, 53 (3): 429–46.

Leahey, C. (2012), 'Angela Ahrendts: The Secrets Behind Burberry's Growth', *Fortune Online*, 19 June 2012. Available online: http://fortune.com/2012/06/19/angela-ahrendts-the-secrets-behind-burberrys-growth/ (accessed 1 October 2014).

Legs from Leeds (2005), *ReviewCentre*, January 2005. Available online: https://www.reviewcentre/review133541.html (accessed 11 March 2022).

Leicester Mercury (2004), 'Pub-Goers Facing "Burberry Ban"', 20 August 2004. Available online: http://news.bbc.co.uk/1/hi/england/leicestershire/3583900.stm (accessed 30 March 2014).

Lury, C. (1996), *Consumer Culture*, Cambridge: Polity.

Lury, C. (2004), *Brands: The Logos of the Global Economy*, London: Routledge.

Lury, C. and Moor, L. (2010), 'Brand Valuation and Topological Culture', in
    M. Aronczyk and D. Powers (eds), *Blowing Up the Brand*, New York: Peter Lang.
Madeley, G. (2003), 'Casual Elegance Leads to Burberry Ban in City Pubs', *Daily Mail*,
    12 November 2003. Available online: http://www.highbeam.com/doc/1G1-110120
    961.html (accessed 2 July 2014).
Manovich, L. (2006), 'The Poetics of Augmented Space', London, Thousand Oaks, CA,
    New Delhi: Sage.
Marzano, S. (2000), 'Branding = Distinctive Authenticity', in J. Pavitt (ed.) *Brand. New*,
    London: V&A.
Mauss, M. (1950), *The Gift: The Form and Reason for Exchange in Archaic Societies*,
    New York: W. W. Norton.
May, C. and Sell, S. (2005), *Intellectual Property Rights: A Critical History*, Boulder:
    Lynne Riener.
McClintock, A. (1995), *Imperial Leather: Race, Gender and Sexuality in the Colonial
    Conquest*, Oxford: Routledge.
McCraken, G. (1988), *Culture and Consumption: New Approaches to the Symbolic
    Character of Consumer Goods and Activities*, Bloomington: Indiana University Press.
McKenzie, S. (2013), 'Angela Ahrendts: The Burberry CEO Who Reinvented a Heritage
    Brand for the Digital Age', CNN, 15 October 2013. Available online: http://edit
    ion.cnn.com/2013/10/15/business/the-burberry-ceo-who-reinvented/ (accessed 6
    May 2014).
McLuhan, M. and Fiore, Q. (2005), *The Medium Is the Message: An Inventory of Effects*,
    Berkeley: Ginkgo Press.
Mellor, A. (1991), 'Enterprise and Heritage In the Dock', *Enterprise and Heritage:
    Crosscurrents of National Culture*, London: Routledge.
Menkes, S. (2002), 'Building British Luxury Brands: Bravo! Reburnished Burberry
    Sets the Pace', *New York Times Online*, 10 September 2002. Available online: http://
    www.nytimes.com/2002/09/10/style/10iht-burberry_ed3_.html (accessed 6
    November 2013).
Mesure, S. (2004), ' "Chav" Link Has Affected Demand, Says Burberry', *The Independent*,
    14 October 2004. Available online: http://www.independent.co.uk/news/business/
    news/chav-link-has-affected-demand-says-burberry-6160099.html (accessed 3
    March 2013).
Miller, D. (1998), *A Theory of Shopping*, Oxford: Polity.
Milligan, L. (2012), 'Burberry Up', *British Vogue Online*, 23 May 2012. Available
    online: http://www.vogue.co.uk/news/2012/05/23/burberry-sales-and-prof
    its-end-of-year-2011 (accessed 8 October 2014).
Mills, L. (2000), 'Bravo for Burberry', *The Telegraph Online*, 9 July 2000. Available
    online: http://www.telegraph.co.uk/finance/personalfinance/comment/4457553/
    Bravo-for-Burberry.html (accessed 24 February 2014).
Mod-to-Suedehead Style Forum. Available online: https://www.styleforum.net/threads/
    mod-to-suedehead.89027/ (accessed 31 March 2015).

Moor, L. (2007), *The Rise of Brands*, Oxford: Berg.

Moore, C. M. and Birtwistle, G. (2004), 'The Burberry Business Model: Creating an International Luxury Fashion Brand', *International Journal of Retail & Distribution Management*, 32 (8): 412–22.

Morton, C. (2006), 'Burberry Prorsum A-W 2006–07', *British Vogue*, 23 February 2006. Available online: http://www.vogue.co.uk/fashion/autumn-winter-2006/ready-to-wear/burberry-prorsum (accessed 1 October 2014).

Mort, F. (1996), *Cultures of Consumption: Commerce, Masculinities and Social Space*, Abingdon: Routledge.

Moth, D. (2013), 'How Burberry Uses Facebook, Twitter, Pinterest and Google+', *Econsultancy*, 12 June 2013. Available online: https://econsultancy.com/blog/62897-how-burberry-uses-facebook-twitter-pinterest-and-google#i.1qtk1r7 17p0drx (accessed 7 October 2014).

Mower, S. (2001), 'Vogue View London Report: Burberry's Blue-Eyed Boy', *British Vogue*, 1 September 2001: 408.

Mower, S. (2002), 'Burberry Prorsum Spring–Summer Ready-to-Wear', *Style.com*, 30 September 2002. Available online: http://www.style.com/fashion-shows/spring-2003-ready-to-wear/burberry-prorsum (accessed 23 September 2014).

Mower, S. (2006), 'Burberry Prorsum Fall 2007 Ready-to-Wear', *Style.com*, 19 February 2007. Available online: https://www.vogue.com/fashion-shows/fall-2007-ready-to-wear/burberry-prorsum (accessed 1 October 2014).

Mower, S (2010), 'Burberry Prorsum: Fall 2010 Ready-to-Wear, *Style.com*, 22 February 2010. Available online: http://www.style.com/fashionshows/review/F2010RTW-BURBERRY (accessed 2 September 2014).

Nava, M. (1987), 'Consumerism and Its Contradictions', *Cultural Studies*, 1 (2): 204–10.

Nava, M. (1998), 'The Cosmopolitanism of Commerce and the Allure of Difference: Selfridges, the Russian Ballet and the Tango 1911–1914, *International Journal of Cultural Studies, Sage*, 1(2): 163–96.

Nava, M. (2007), *Visceral Cosmopolitanism: Gender, Culture and the Normalization of Difference*, Oxford: Berg.

Nava, M. (2008), 'Shopping for England', *BBC2 Television*, 24 November 2008. Available online: http://www.bbc.co.uk/programmes/b0074tpn (accessed 4 March 2013).

Neate, R. (2013). 'How an American Woman Rescued Burberry, a Classic British Label', *The Observer Online*, 16 June 2013. Available online: http://www.theguardian.com/business/2013/jun/16/angela-ahrendts-burberry-chav-image (accessed 6 May 2014).

Nixon, S. (1997) 'Exhibiting Masculinity', in S. Hall (ed.), *Representation: Cultural Representation and Signifying Practices*, London: Sage, 170–90.

Oldfart (2004), *ReviewCentre*, December 2004. Available online: https://www.reviewcentre.com/review133541.html.

Olins, A. (2008), 'Goodies that Gained Global Sales', *The Times*, 29 May 2008: 25.

Olins, A. (2009), 'After the Goldrush', *The Times T2*, 21 January 2009: 12.

Olins, W. (1978), *The Corporate Personality: An Enquiry into the Nature of Corporate Identity*, London: Design Council.

Olins, W. (2008), *The Brand Handbook*, London: Thames and Hudson.

Oliver, M. (2004), 'I Don't Care If You Are Tony Blair, You're Not Coming in Dressed Like That', 21 August 2004. Available online: https://www.theguardian.com/polit ics/2004/aug/21/clothes.politics (accessed 30 March 2014).

Partington, A. (1992), 'Popular Fashion and Working Class Affluence', in J. Ash and E. Wilson (eds), *Chic Thrills*, London: HarperCollins.

Phipps, B. (2009), 'Burberry and Facebook Make "Art of the Trench"', *Brands Create Customers*, 9 November 2009. Available online: http://tenayagroup.com/ blog/2009/11/10/burberry-and-facebook-make-art-of-the-trench/http://tena yagroup.com/blog/2009/11/10/burberry-and-facebook-make-art-of-the-trench/ (accessed 5 September 2014).

Picardie, J. (2006), 'Bailey's Original', *British Vogue*, February 2006: 175–9.

Pilditch, J. (1970), *Communication by Design: A Study in Corporate Identity*, New York: McGraw Hill.

Pike, A. (2011), 'Placing Brands and Branding: A Socio-Spatial Biography of Newcastle Brown Ale', *Transactions of the Institute of British Geographers*, 36(2): 206–22.

Police Specials Forum (2004). Available online: http://www.policespecials.com/forum/ index.php/topic/14481-pubs-ban-burberry/ (accessed 7 May 2015).

Porter, C. (2007), 'BoomBox: The Club that Inspired a Fashion Phenomenon', *The Independent Online*, 16 September 2007. Available online: http://www.independent. co.uk/news/uk/this-britain/boombox-the-london-club-that-inspired-a-fashion-phe nomenon-402352.html (accessed 2 July 2014).

Porter, M. E. (2004), *Competitive Advantage: Creating and Sustaining Superior Performance*, New York: Free Press.

PR Web (Gracia Arnico) (2007), 'Burberry Launches Autumn–Winter 2007 Advertising campaign', 7 July 2007. Available online: https://www.prweb.com/releases/2007/07/ prweb537822.html (accessed 15 March 2014).

Publican, The (2003), 'Call for Discretion Over Burberry Ban', *Morning Advertiser*, 18 November 2003. Available online: http://www.morningadvertiser.co.uk/Gene ral-News/Aberdeen-pub-bans-Burberry (accessed 8 March 2022).

Real Football Factories (2006). Available online: https://docur.co/documentary/ the-real-football-factories (accessed 25 June 2014).

Review Centre (2004), 1 September. Available online: http://www.reviewcentre.com/ reviews52540.html (accessed 14 August 2013).

Ritzer, G. (1993), *The McDonaldization of Society*, Thousand Oaks, CA: Sage in C. Lury (2004), *Brands: The Logos of the Global Economy*, London: Routledge.

Robertson, S. (2004), 'Pub Bans Drinkers Wearing Luxury Clothing Brands', *PR Week*, 3 September 2004. Available online: https://www.prweek.com/article/220759/ pubs-ban-drinkers-wearing-luxury-clothing-brands (accessed 30 March 2014).

Robins, K. (1991), 'Tradition and Translation: National Culture in Its Global Context', in Corner and Harvey (eds), *Enterprise and Heritage: Crosscurrents of National Culture*, London: Routledge.

Rohwedder, C. (2008), 'Burberry Looks to Retrench', *Wall Street Journal Online*, 18 November 2008. Available online: http://online.wsj.com/news/articles/SB1226995 39412236779 (accessed 4 September 2014).

Royle, T. (2000), *Working for McDonald's in Europe: The Unequal Struggle?*, London: Routledge.

Sander, D. (2014), 'How Brands Invest in Music, *feature.fm*, 29 September 2014, Available online: http://www.feature.fm/blog/brands-music/ (accessed 7 October 2014).

Sartorialist, The (2009), 'Biography'. Available online: http://www.thesartorialist.com/ biography/ (accessed 4 September 2014).

Sawers, A. (2007), 'Stacey Cartwright, Chief Financial Officer, Burberry Plc', *Financial Director (Features and Interviews)*, 25 January 2007. Available online: http://www. financialdirector.co.uk/financial-director/feature/1742669/stacey-cartwright-chief-financial-officer-burberry-plc (accessed 2 October 2014).

Seares, E. (2010), 'Burberry to Launch "Runway to Reality" In-Store Event During LFW', *Drapers*, 9 September 2010. Available online: https://www.drapersonline.com/ news/burberry-to-launch-runway-to-reality-in-store-event-during-lfw (accessed 24 September 2014).

Secularcafé.org (2011a), 23 January 2011. Available online: http://www.secularcafe.org/ showthread.php?t=10442 (accessed 21 July 2015).

Secularcafé.org (2011b), 26 January 2011.

Seidler, B. (2013), 'I.T.s in the Bag', *New York Times Online*, 18 February 2013. Available online: https://www.nytimes.com/2013/02/19/fashion/at-burberry-its-in-the-bag. html (accessed 26 September 2013).

Shin, S. (2012), 'What Burberry is Doing Right that Other Luxury Retailers are Not', *CNBC*, 17 January 2012. Available online: http://www.cnbc.com/id/46024993 (accessed 4 Ocotber 2013).

Skeggs, B. (1993), 'Two Minute Brother: Contestation Through Gender, "Race", and Sexuality', *Innovation: The European Journal of Social Sciences*, 6 (3): 299–322.

Skeggs, B. (1997), *Formations of Class and Gender: Becoming Respectable*, London: Sage.

Skeggs, B. (2005), 'Making of Class and Gender through Visualizing Moral Subject Formation', *Sociology*, 39 (5): 965–82.

Skeggs, B. and Woods, H. (2008), 'The Labour Transformation and Circuits of Value "around" Reality Television', *Continuum: Journal of Media and Cultural Studies*, 22 (4): 559–72.

Skey, M. (2011), *National Belonging and Everyday Life: The Significance of Nationhood in an Uncertain World*, London and New York: Palgrave Macmillan.

'Pubs Slap Ban On Burberry Lager Louts' (2004), *Sky News*. Available online: https://news.sky.com/story/291389/pubs-slap-ban-on-burberry-lager-louts (accessed 2 July 2014).

Slater, D. (1997), *Consumer Culture and Modernity*, Oxford: Polity.

Smith, O. (2013), 'Burberry Weaves its Magic into a New Pattern of Thought', *CrowdMedia*, 18 April 2013. Available online: http://crowdmedia.co.uk/blogposts/burberry-weaves-its-magic-into-a-new-pattern-of-thought/ (accessed 7 October 2014).

Sonne, P. (2011), 'Mink or Fox? The Trench Gets Complicated', *Wall Street Journal Online*, 3 November 2011. Available online: http://www.wsj.com/articles/SB10001424052970203804204577013842801187070 (accessed 22 April 2015).

Soudager, R. (2013), 'How Fashion Retailer Burberry Keeps Customers Coming Back for More', *Forbes*, 28 October 2013. Available online: https://www.forbes.com/sites/sap/2013/10/28/how-fashion-retailer-burberry-keeps-customers-coming-back-for-more/ (accessed 22 April 2015).

Sowray, B. (2012), 'Burberry Awarded £63 Million in Counterfeiting Case', *The Telegraph Online*, 18 May 2012. Available online: http://fashion.telegraph.co.uk/article/TMG9274383/Burberry-awarded-63-million-in-counterfeiting-case.html (accessed 6 March 2013).

Spence, S. (2012), *The Stone Roses: War and Peace*, London: Penguin.

Sunday Times Magazine (1971), 'Meet the Crombie Boys', *Network54*, 28 March 1971. Available online: http://www.loiremagblog.wordpress.com/2013/03/06/meet-the-crombie-boys/ (accessed 25 June 2014).

Sweney, M. (2007), 'Burberry Aims to Check Bad Press', *The Guardian Online*, 1 June 2007. Available online: http://www.theguardian.com/business/2007/jun/01/marketingandpr.media (accessed 12 June 2014).

Telegraph (2004a), 'Pubs Ban Drinkers Dressed in Burberry', 20 August 2004. Available online: http://www.telegraph.co.uk/news/1469814/Pubs-ban-drinkers-dressed-in-Burberry.html (accessed 2 July 2014).

Telegraph (2004b), 'Luxury Brands Fight "Made in EU"' Label', 19 January 2004. Available online: http://www.telegraph.co.uk/finance/2874467/Luxury-brands-fight-Made-in-EU-label.html (accessed 14 May 2014).

Terms and Conditions (n.d.), Art of the Trench http://artofthetrench.burberry.com/guidelines/ (accessed 11 March 2015).

Thrift, N. (2005), 'Movement Space: The Changing Domain of Thinking Arising from the Development of New Forms of Spatial Awareness', *Economy and Society* 33: 582–604.

Time Out (2006), 'Bez on Kate Moss', *Time Out Editors*, 3 August 2006. Available online: http://www.timeout.com/london/music/bez-on-kate-moss-2 (accessed 4 February 2014).

Treadwell, J. (2008), 'Call the [Fashion] Police: How Fashion Became Criminalized', *British Criminology Conference*, 8: 117–33.

Trebay, G. (2012), 'The Garbo of Fashion', *New York Times*, 2 November 2012. Available online: http://www.nytimes.com/2012/11/04/fashion/a-few-words-with-kate-moss-fashions-garbo.html?pagewanted=all&_r=0 (accessed 2 April 2014).

Trend Hunter (2009), 'Burberry Prorsum Men's RTW Fall 2009 at Milan Fashion Week', *Trendhunter*, 19 January 2009. Available online: http://www.trendhunter.com/trends/burberry-prorsum-men-rtw-fall-2009-milan-fashion-week (accessed 19 September 2013).

Turow, J. (2006), 'A Major Transformation', *Niche Envy: Marketing Discrimination in the Digital Age,* Cambridge, MA: MIT Press, 1–19. Available online: http://repository.upenn.edu/asc_papers/132 (accessed 3 November 2012).

Tyler, I. and Bennett, B. (2010), 'Celebrity Chav: Fame, Femininity and Social Class', *European Journal of Cultural Studies*, 13 (3): 375–93.

Tynan, J. (2011), 'Military Dress and Men's Outdoor Leisurewear: Burberry's Trench Coat in First World War Britain', *Journal of Design History*, 24 (2): 139–56.

Veblen, T. (1899), *The Theory of the Leisure Class*, New York: Dover.

Vernon, P. (2006), 'The Fall and Rise of Kate Moss', *The Guardian Online*, 14 May 2006. Available online: http://www.theguardian.com/lifeandstyle/2006/may/14/features.woman6 (accessed 2 April 2014).

Vogue archives (n.d.). Available online: http://www.vogue.com/fashion-shows/designer/burberry-prorsum (accessed 11 March 2022).

Vogue, British (2003), 'Burberry Banned', 12 November 2003. Available online: http://www.vogue.co.uk/news/2003/11/12/burberry-banned (accessed 2 July 2014).

Vogue, British (2004), 'Burberry Prorsum Autumn–Winter Ready to Wear', March 2004. Available online: http://www.vogue.co.uk/fashion/autumn-winter-2004/ready-to-wear/burberry-prorsum (accessed 18 September 2014).

Wang, C. (2014), 'What Do Punks, Streakers, Army Officers, & You Have In Common?', *Refinery29*, 23 November 2014. Available online: http://www.refinery29.com/trench-coat-outfits#slide (accessed 5 March 2015).

Warburton, S. (2011), 'Burberry's Twitter Takeover', *The Telegraph*, 28 September 2011. Available online: http://fashion.telegraph.co.uk/news-features/TMG8793974/Burberrys-Twitter-takeover.html (accessed 3 October 2014).

Warburton, S. (2014), 'Trench Coats: Buy Now, Wear Forever', *The Telegraph*, 5 November 2014. Available online: http://fashion.telegraph.co.uk/article/TMG11205243/Trench-coats-Buy-Now-Wear-Forever.html (accessed 5 March 2015).

Watts, P. (2007), 'Death of the Cockney', *Time Out Online*, 2 July 2007. Available online: http://www.timeout.com/london/things-to-do/death-of-the-cockney-1 (accessed 15 September 2015).

Wemyss, G. (2009), *The Invisible Empire: White Discourse, Tolerance and Belonging* London: Ashgate.

Weston, S. (2009), 'Can Craft Make You Happy?', *Crafts Council*, Spark Plug Curator's Award. Available online: http://www.sianweston.org.uk/research (accessed 10 September 2010).

Wildlife Guardian (2002). Available online: https://www.wildlifeguardian.co.uk/hunt
ing/quotes/ (accessed 11 March 2022).

Wilson, E. (1988), *Adorned in Dreams: Fashion and Modernity*, London: I.B. Taurus.

Wilson, E. (2005), 'Amid Drug Use Reports, 2 More Brands Drop Kate Moss', *New York Times*, 22 September 2005. Available online: https://www.nytimes.com/2005/09/22/
business/media/amid-drug-use-reports-2-more-brands-drop-kate-moss.html
(accessed 17 April 2014).

Williams, E. (2012), 'Heritage Meets Digital in New Flagship Burberry Store',
Creative Review Online, 14 September 2012. Available online: http://www.cre
ativereview.co.uk/cr-blog/2012/september/burberry-mixes-heritage-with-digi
tal-high-tech-in-new-london-store (accessed 9 April 2015).

Williamson, C. (2013), 'Burberry Anti-Social on Social Media', *Big Group*, July 2013.
Available online: http://www.biggroup.co.uk/en/blog/burberry-anti-social-on-soc
ial-media (accessed 24 April 2015).

Williamson, J. (1978), *Decoding Advertisements: Ideology and Meaning in Advertising*,
London: Marion Boyars.

World of Kays: A Lifetime in Fashion and Style (2011), *University of Worcester*.
Available online: http://www.worldofkays.org (accessed 4 February 2014).

Wright Mills, C. (2000), *The Sociological Imagination*, Oxford: Oxford University Press.

Wright, P. (1985), *On Living in an Old Country: National Past in Contemporary Britain*,
London: Verso.

YouTube (GB) (2012a), 'Midnight Rain' – The Burberry A/W12 Campaign ', *YouTube*,
8 June 2012. Available online: https://www.youtube.com/watch?v=UVuZQrPe
BLg&list=PL_YRf89haPlEnQ7DCtS-N5c-3c4NqPwOB (accessed 6 November
2013).

YouTube (2012b), 'Craftsmanship: Burberry Tailoring', *YouTube*, 7 March 2012.
Available online: https://www.youtube.com/watch?v=_phxLpmf3QY (accessed 7
March 2013).

Index

Ahrendts, Angela 4, 6, 8, 43–5, 47–9, 72, 113, 130
America(n), North America 4, 16, 17, 29, 41, 51, 56, 58–9, 63–4, 68, 71, 130
Aquascutum 9, 33, 82
archive 2, 14, 16
aristocracy 59, 64, 127, 135, 153
  aristocratic adventurer 5–6, 43
authenticity 135, 144

bad object 91, 93
  bad consumer 4, 7
Bailey, Christopher 1, 41–2, 45, 94, 127
Beijing, Burberry Beijing 6, 44–5
Berardi, Antonio 136
Blair, Tony 43, 65
Bloomsbury Group 5, 127, 129, 163
Blow, Isabella 56, 59
Bohemian 127
Bond Street (London) 47, 64, 115, 126, 154
branding 29, 52, 55, 66, 159, 162
  rebranding 8, 49, 55–6, 58, 64, 71, 99, 162
Bravo, Rose Marie 4, 6–8, 37–8, 41, 43, 44–47, 49, 52–3, 55–6, 59, 63–5, 68–73, 77–8, 88, 99, 101, 126, 130–1, 154, 159, 160, 163
British 1, 4, 5–6, 8–9, 13, 16, 18, 21, 24, 28–9, 31, 33, 35, 38, 40–1, 43, 45, 48, 52–3, 58–9, 61–2, 68, 71, 78, 80–2, 86, 93, 99–101, 117, 123, 126, 129, 131–3, 135, 137, 141, 147, 149–53, 155, 159–63
  actor(s) 6, 38, 40
  class system 1, 38, 68, 70, 78, 98
  economy 24, 125
  culture 21, 31, 62, 66, 68, 90
  government 13, 24, 103
  imperial power 5, 18
  lifestyle 130

  national identity 4–63
Britishness 1–2, 4, 6, 43, 49, 56, 59, 63, 66, 68, 70–2, 123, 125, 135, 156, 159–60, 164
Burberry
  Acoustic 5, 42, 48–9, 149–50
  Art of the Trench 5, 46–7, 138–40, 143, 145, 149, 156, 160–1
  Chicago 139
  Prorsum 41, 48, 88, 133, 136, 142
  Runway to Reality 5, 46, 49, 143, 145, 149
  Warrior handbag 8, 122–3
Burnett, Mervyn (*see also* GMB) 108, 121

capital
  cultural 65, 76, 84, 94, 98, 100
  economic 65, 98
  educational 80
  symbolic 80
celebrity 11, 91, 93, 95
  celebrity endorsement 5, 162
  'chav', celebrity 'chav' 7, 84, 85–7, 90, 91, 93–5, 100, 163
China, Chinese 6, 44, 45, 51, 89, 103, 116, 122, 159
class
  British class system 1, 38
  hierarchy 7, 68, 78, 164
  middle class 16, 31, 53, 81, 85–6, 89, 94, 98, 127, 163
  working class 81, 86, 94, 98, 163
conservative government 52, 85, 125
consumerism 5, 29, 48, 80, 96
consumption 1, 4, 7, 14, 21, 37, 48–9, 101, 160, 163
  contested 1
  working class 40, 63, 84, 87, 91, 162, 163
Country Life magazine 29, 127
Cool Britannia 38, 51, 64–5, 71

counterfeit, counterfeiting,
    counterfeiters 6, 33, 38, 48–9, 87–90,
    99, 100, 130, 141
craft skills 3, 112
Crombie, Crombie boys (*see also* suede
    heads) 80–1

Daks 80
Dancy, Hugh 5, 38–40, 129
Day, Corrine 56
department store 16–18, 75
de-skilling 7
Deyn, Agyness 4, 123, 133–4
diffusion 1, 164
Donaldson, Lily 4 -5, 127–8, 134, 136, 137

eccentricity 70, 71, 159
economy 5, 24, 41, 97, 118, 130, 135, 145
    British 24, 125
    Chinese 44
    Global 5, 130, 155
English Country Gent (*see also* Stewart,
    Rod) 80, 163
English Heritage 44
exports 33

Facebook 8, 46, 49, 138–40, 147,
    150, 152–3
factory, factory workers 2, 104–5, 107, 109,
    112, 115, 121
fakes (*see also* counterfeiting and grey
    market) 7, 88–90, 98–100
Ferry
    Bryan 43
    Isaac 43, 159
    Otis 43, 159
fictional historic character(s) 38

gender, gendered 7, 17, 56, 72, 95, 97, 100,
    109, 111, 162–3
GMB, Britain's general union (*see also*
    Burnett, Mervyn) 106–10, 115–16
Gormley, Keira 134
grey market (*see also* fakes and
    counterfeiting) 6, 130

Hampshire, Cultural Trust, Hampshire
    Museum Services 2, 9, 11, 19, 24
Hansard 21–2

heritage 1, 4–5, 8, 51, 116, 123, 125–7,
    129–33, 135–8, 141, 143–7,
    149–57, 160–4
    heritage mythology 8
heroin chic 58

identity 3, 4–6, 13, 29, 37, 52, 56, 59, 63,
    69, 78, 81, 92, 97, 126
    brand, corporate 4, 29, 52, 59, 126, 145
    classed 99, 163
    creative 71
    cultural 1
    fashioned 55
    group, shared 1, 3, 78, 81, 82
    online 160
Instagram 8, 149–50, 152–5

labour 1, 4, 7–8, 42, 48, 105, 111, 116, 118,
    120, 137, 156, 162, 164
    contested labour, exploited labour 22,
    115, 141, 161
labour government, New Labour 5, 38,
    53, 65, 85
lawlessness 4, 62, 159
licensing 33, 38, 88, 131
Lichfield, Lord 31
luxury 1–8, 33, 35, 37, 40, 44, 46, 51, 54–5,
    62–3, 66, 69, 73, 77–8, 82, 84–5,
    88–90, 100, 103, 108, 110–11, 115,
    121, 126, 130–1, 140, 146, 149, 153,
    155–6, 161, 163–4

Madchester 61, 64–5, 69, 71
mail order catalogue 4, 53, 74–7, 81,
    99, 112
military officers 11, 13, 34
millennial(s) 1, 130, 149
Mods 80, 90, 96, 162
Monarchy, British 29, 31, 137
moral panic 4, 7, 41, 49, 78, 81, 94, 163
Moss, Kate 4, 6–7, 41–3, 49, 51–2, 58–9,
    61–2, 58–74, 78, 99, 125, 159

nation state 72, 159
nationalism 72
    banal nationalism 72
    hybrid national identity 6, 56, 125
    nationalistic dream 72
nationhood 13, 7

new man 40
nostalgia 133, 136–7, 141, 143

party-loving 70, 159
patrician 59, 61, 70, 159
Pearly King 4, 66, 68, 71
Pinterest 8, 150, 152, 155
product placement 5, 162

Queen Elizabeth ll 31
  coronation 1953, 29–31

respectable, dis-respectable,
    respectability 7, 85–7, 94, 99, 133, 163
Ross, Liberty 74
rural idyll 42, 135, 137

Scuttlers 78, 81–2, 84
service sector 5, 35, 125, 138
Shackleton, Sir Ernest 5, 14–15, 43, 135
social networking (*see also* Facebook,
    Instagram, Pinterest, Twitter) 91,
    151, 154–6
souvenir 8, 19, 66, 152, 157
Stewart, Rod (*see also* English Country
    Gent) 78, 80
suede heads (*see also* Crombie Boys) 80–81

tastemakers 4, 44, 160
Tennant, Stella 4, 6, 42–3, 56–60, 70–2,
    159, 162–3
Testino, Mario 40, 56, 63, 125

thrift 3–4, 22, 76, 120, 163
traditions, traditional 33, 42–4, 66, 68,
    70–2, 75, 77, 80, 84–5, 97, 130, 138,
    143, 145, 149, 151, 156, 160, 162
  British tradition 43, 59
transgression, transgressive 7, 74
Treorchy 3–4, 7–8, 101, 103–6, 108–13,
    115–18, 120–3, 161–2
Twitter 8, 46, 49, 146–7, 150, 152–5
  tweet walk 146, 151, 153, 155

underpenetrated markets 6, 159

value, values 4–6, 14, 28–9, 34–5, 37–8,
    41, 46, 53–6, 59, 61, 76, 86, 94, 99,
    126, 131, 140, 143, 147, 154, 156,
    160, 162–3
  economic 65, 70–72, 74, 86–8, 95, 100,
    122–3, 133, 139, 145–6
  ethical 68, 70, 90, 98, 122, 159
Vogue, British 41, 51, 59, 68, 71, 82, 127,
    131, 136–7, 143

Walpole, (luxury lobby group) 66
Ward, Gemma 132
Woolf, Virginia 127
World Cup '98 3
whimsical, whimsy 33, 63, 71
Wilde, Gabriella 125–6, 150–2, 163
Windsor, Duke and Duchess 5, 131, 163

Zulu Warriors 81–2, 84, 162

www.ingramcontent.com/pod-product-compliance
Lightning Source LLC
Chambersburg PA
CBHW050446280326
41932CB00013BA/2262